The Euro as Politics

The Euro as Politics

The Euro as Politics

PEDRO SCHWARTZ

The Institute of Economic Affairs

First published in Great Britain in 2004 by
The Institute of Economic Affairs
2 Lord North Street
Westminster
London SW1P 3LB
in association with Profile Books Ltd

The mission of the Institute of Economic Affairs is to improve public understanding of the fundamental institutions of a free society, with particular reference to the role of markets in solving economic and social problems.

A CIP catalogue record for this book is available from the British Library.

ISBN 0 255 36535 7

Many IEA publications are translated into languages other than English or are reprinted. Permission to translate or to reprint should be sought from the Director General at the address above.

Typeset in Stone by MacGuru Ltd
info@macguru.org.uk

Printed and bound in Great Britain by Hobbs the Printers

CONTENTS

THE AUTHOR

Professor Pedro Schwartz was educated at the Compluten-sian University of Madrid, where he graduated and obtained a doctorate in law. He also gained an MSc (Econ.) and a PhD in political science at the London School of Economics.

His academic career includes a period at the Bentham Project at University College, London, a chair in the history of economic thought at the Complutensian University of Madrid and then at the Autonomous University of Madrid, and lately a professorship in economics at the Universidad San Pablo CEU of Madrid. He also lectures at the Madrid Campus of St Louis University, Missouri. He has published in the fields of economics, history and political philosophy, and is well known as a contributor to Spanish and British newspapers.

He worked for ten years as an economist in the research department of the Bank of Spain. From 1982 to 1986 he was a Spanish Conservative MP, and for the following fifteen years chief economist for a Madrid Stock Exchange broker, then chairman of a fund management company. At present he is a director of Foreign & Colonial Eurotrust PLC. He also is on the board of the IT consulting company DMR Spain and chairs MTS Spain, a virtual bond market.

In September 1990, HM Queen Elizabeth II made Professor Schwartz an honorary Officer of the British Empire. He has just been elected a member of the Real Academia de Ciencias Morales y Políticas of Spain and awarded the Jaime I Prize for economics.

To the memory of Lionel Robbins,
teacher and friend

FOREWORD

The Euro as Politics sheds new light on the discussions within the UK on the subject of whether or not to adopt the euro as our currency. Although Professor Schwartz questions the main political and economic arguments used on both sides of the debate, he develops a consistent free-market position that suggests that there are considerable dangers to the UK in adopting the euro.

Professor Schwartz reviews the economic arguments for and against the euro dispassionately. His views may not make happy reading for free-market, anti-euro economists, however. Schwartz argues that, in a free economy with low regulation, it matters little what currency is used because relative prices and wages in any currency will generally adjust to changing economic conditions. The arguments that are used by free-market economists to criticise the use of monetary policy to increase economic growth are the same as the ones that can be used to dismiss the idea that a separate domestic currency is necessary to deal with 'asymmetric shocks'.

The economic arguments frequently used by the 'pro-euro' camp do not stand up to close scrutiny either, according to Schwartz. The thesis that the adoption of the euro will increase trade and reduce currency volatility is unproven at best. This all means, argues Schwartz, that the economic debate surrounding the Chancellor of the Exchequer's five economic tests is largely irrelevant.

The political arguments for and against joining the euro are not regarded as especially important by the British government, although many individuals, on either side of the debate, do stress political issues. Again, Schwartz finds the particular issues that are used in the debate unconvincing. To a liberal economist, should the concept of political sovereignty be important? Surely, Schwartz suggests, we should want international and national political arrangements that best guarantee economic and political freedom. But many of the free-market opponents of the euro in the UK seem wedded to the ideal of national political sovereignty.

That Schwartz is so critical of many of the received arguments for and against the euro does not mean that he is indifferent. He is fundamentally sympathetic to the euro and very sympathetic towards a European Union built on free trade, free capital movements and the free movement of labour. Schwartz finds, however, that there are economic arguments for keeping sterling that, while not decisive, certainly provide a prima facie case for not joining the euro. Therefore, to find a decisive argument, one needs to look at the political issues.

While traditional political arguments for and against the euro are found wanting, there are strong political arguments for keeping sterling. The most fundamental of these is institutional competition. The record of government-controlled central banks in maintaining the value of the currency is a very poor one. In the 250 years between the Bank of England being founded and it being nationalised, one pound sterling lost about two-thirds of its value, and most of this loss of value came in wartime. In the sixty years since the Bank of England was nationalised, one pound sterling has lost 96 per cent of its value. The ideal, surely, would be to have a competitive market or a contestable market in the provision of money. But that is not on the agenda. Our author suggests that, given the circumstances in which we find ourselves, 'institutional competition' is very healthy for both the ECB and the Bank of England. Both operate in pretty good institutional and legal frameworks. It is hard to escape the conclusion, however, that those frameworks are more likely to remain sound if the institutions have to compete with and can learn from each other. Legal tender laws should be abolished, of course, to ensure proper competition between sterling and the euro and between the institutions that underpin the currencies.

It is then possible to generalise from this argument. Institutional competition would be helpful elsewhere in the EU. We should have free trade and not uniform regulations; in areas such as financial services, we should recognise each other's rules rather than trying to harmonise regulations. Overall, we can paint a picture of a European Union with less conflict – because there will be less that countries have to agree on. It will also be a European Union with a higher degree of prosperity and competition because institutional competition should lead to less regulation as politicians – who have a vested interest in regulation – will be more restrained.

Thus the conclusion of *The Euro as Politics* can be applied not only to the issue of whether the UK adopts the euro but also to the issue of whether the UK adopts the conclusions of the Constitutional Convention. Adopting the euro and adopting the proposals of the Convention would take the EU in the wrong direction, it is argued.

The proof of Schwartz's argument would arise if, a few decades after the UK joins the euro, the ECB has debased the currency, perhaps to facilitate the financing of the huge burden of unfunded pension liabilities. Considering this possibility, Schwartz's argument becomes very compelling. If sterling still existed such a move would hardly affect the British people. But Continentals could also avoid the damaging effects by using sterling themselves. More importantly, because individuals could switch currencies in an environment of currency competition, the ECB would have little to gain from inflation and would be restrained from creating it in the first place. There would be no such constraints in a Europe of monopoly money.

The views expressed in Research Monograph 58 are, as in all IEA publications, those of the author and not those of the Institute (which has no corporate view), its managing trustees, Academic Advisory Council members or senior staff.

PHILIP BOOTH

Editorial and Programme Director,
Institute of Economic Affairs
Professor of Insurance and Risk Management,
Sir John Cass Business School, City University
May 2004

SUMMARY

- The euro has clear advantages for member states with a tradition of monetary instability and unsound finances. It also tightens their links to the EU and helps them overcome their authoritarian past.
- The British economy does not need the euro because the Bank of England manages the currency well, monetary union has no measurable effects on trade and investment, and, by keeping sterling, Britain can avoid the hidden liability of unfunded pensions that may tempt the ECB to create inflation.
- It is a myth that, by joining the euro, Britain will reduce exchange rate risk. This myth arises because too little consideration is given to the issues of exchange rate volatility against the dollar and of 'real' rather than 'nominal' exchange rate flexibility.
- While the above economic issues are important they are not decisive. The economic arguments for and against the euro are not a 'life and death issue'. The particular economic arguments that are important are, in any case, not generally the arguments that are considered in the Chancellor of the Exchequer's five tests.
- Giving up sterling for the euro is not so much an economic as a political question. The economic case would have to be very strong to overwhelm the political arguments.

- Monetary unions have never lasted without the backing of a central authority and therefore the euro needs a political authority to back it.
- In a world of state currencies, monetary competition with free movement of capital is the best safeguard against inflation.
- The pound serves a useful political function in the UK and an essential one in the whole of the EU since it will foster institutional variety, limit the concentration of power, restrain enforced harmonisation and, as a result, favour individual autonomy.
- Because the arguments relating to currency competition and preventing the development of centralised political power are so important, the British answer in a referendum on the euro could change the course of European history, for good or bad.
- The arguments relating to the sterling-versus-euro debate are one part of an important general approach to EU politics. The UK should promote competition and not harmonisation within a free European Union. That competition should apply to regulatory systems and currencies.

TABLES, FIGURES AND BOXES

Tables

Figures

Boxes

INTRODUCTION:
THE PUZZLE OF THE EURO

*The problems raised by a conscious direction of economic affairs
on a national scale inevitably assume even greater dimensions
when the same is attempted internationally.*

HAYEK, IN *THE ROAD TO SERFDOM*, 1944

The euro, a bold and stupendous economic experiment, puzzles
many of us Europeans, especially the British, the Danes and the
Swedes, who have for the time being kept their national currencies. What are the costs and benefits, in the short and the long
term, of being a full member of EMU, the Economic and Monetary
Union of the EU? Are the reasons for taking up the euro mainly
economic or really political? To express it more directly, were the
Continental members of the EU right in giving up their central
banks and their monetary sovereignty? Should Sweden, Denmark
and the new candidate nations fully enter the euro zone? Should
Britain give up the pound? Does the euro bode well for Europe and
for the world economy?

The perplexity has been deepened by two developments in the
euro zone and by a government publication in Britain. The two
developments are the lacklustre performance of the euro economies since the launch of the single currency and the apparent
demise of the 'Growth and Stability Pact'. The publication is HM
Treasury's *Assessment of the Five Conditions* – those to be fulfilled

by the UK before fully joining the Economic and Monetary Union (EMU) – a set of eighteen high-quality reports amounting to a total of no fewer than twenty volumes of contradictory evidence and opinion.

The British government's official line is that five conditions have to be fulfilled before adopting the euro:

- *Convergence:* Are business cycles and economic structures compatible so that we and others could live comfortably with euro interest rates on a permanent basis?
- *Flexibility:* If problems emerge is there sufficient flexibility to deal with them?
- *Investment:* Would joining EMU create better conditions for firms making long-term decisions to invest in Britain?
- *Financial services:* What impact would entry into EMU have on the competitive position of the UK's financial services industry, particularly the City's wholesale markets?
- *Growth, stability and employment:* In summary, will joining EMU promote higher growth, stability and a lasting increase in jobs?

To which a sixth condition has lately been added: the *Increase in trade and foreign investment in Britain*.

Once those conditions are met, the government will approve giving up sterling for the euro and will put the question to a consultative referendum.

The Treasury's assessment is so indecisive, however, that it reinforces the widely held suspicion that the real position of the British government is one of 'yes in principle but wait and see for the moment'. This is disingenuous. The question is not one of finding the best painkiller for an operation that must be performed as soon as the conditions are right but *whether* it should be performed at all. The British have a duty to ask this awkward question and claim the right to decide on the apparently inevitable. As a good European and a friend of Britain, I have agonised over this matter for many years. My conclusions in this monograph were certainly not foregone. Anybody with an internationalist bent will be in two minds as to whether monetary sovereignty should be kept or given up.

A number of Continental countries are in fact better off with the new European currency. The euro is expected to be sounder than the lira or peseta or escudo or drachma. The Growth and Stability Pact has prodded them to put their public finances in order. Low inflation and a zero deficit are a short cut to lower interest rates and investor confidence. Should the UK follow the same path? The answer is not immediately clear.

The UK, a relatively flexible economy with good macroeconomic management, does not need the discipline imposed on some other economies. Also, the adaptation cost for the UK could be higher than the benefits of the new monetary regime. Should sterling, itself a pretty sound currency, be given up?

On the other hand, having the euro as a single currency over the whole of the European Union does carry a political message of togetherness. Now that the EU has grown to 25 members, with more likely to follow, with different languages and cultures and dissimilar constitutional traditions, a single currency may create a tiny but needed bond. Is monetary sovereignty vested in the national state not a relic of an insular past?

The first thesis of this monograph is that, from an economic point of view, the kind of money used by individuals and firms in a country is in the long run unimportant, on condition that the currency is stable and monetary policy predictable.

An open market will function with several currencies on offer. The reason is that people have an interest in pulling aside the monetary veil to discover what goods and services really cost, what wages and salaries can really buy, what interest and profits really say about the worth of an investment or a business. And if people have an interest in not being deceived by appearances they will uncover reality – whatever governments and central banks may do. In consequence, a good economist knows that trying to manage the currency to foster growth or increase employment or dampen the cycle is futile at best and harmful at worst.

From an economic point of view, the question is not how to place in the hands of European authorities the best monetary instrument to govern the real economy but how to ensure that Britain and the whole of Europe enjoy a sound currency. The charter of the European Central Bank (ECB) makes a valiant attempt at guaranteeing that its principal goal will be maintaining the value of the euro. But the history of central banks shows that institutional rules of good conduct are transient unless backed by market competition. While the rules of the gold standard were respected and people were ready to bear, and react to, the pain of flexibility, a single currency for the whole world did sterling service for economic freedom. But the euro is not a commodity money, but a fiat money. A belts-and-braces arrangement may be needed, so that competition encourages good behaviour by central bankers.

If a diversity of currencies in the EU is not in itself an obstacle to the smooth functioning of the single market, then currency competition could be an added guarantee that straying central banks and meddlesome governments will be punished. This is not to say that one should try to split existing monetary zones artificially, thus throwing away the information content of existing means of payment: in matters of money (and national borders) prudence is advisable. But should one throw away good currencies when they can be an instrument of choice and competition? The market itself could in the end determine whether the euro would become the more widely used currency in Britain, Scandinavia and Switzerland.

This argument that keeping the pound could contribute to a sound monetary environment in Europe should not be lightly set aside. In any case, it would not be complete without looking at the political dimension of the question.

The second thesis of this monograph is political: that the single currency will reinforce the drive towards European unity, therefore its acceptability depends on what kind of united Europe is being built. The European Union is the result of aspirations of people with different and even contrary aims, and of the unintended consequences of their efforts. As such it is an ambiguous project. The four freedoms of the Treaty of Rome, the freedom of movement of goods, services, capital and people, have brought more liberty for Europeans. The accession of new nations to the EU again implies opening doors and lifting barriers. On the other hand, there are growing moves in Brussels and in some member states towards creating a European bloc, towards building an old-style European nanny state in place of the failing national welfare states. The signs are worrying: interfering regulations excused in terms of imposing economic freedom; continuous calls for tax harmonisation and economic convergence; a mountainous 'acquis communautaire' of never-repealed legislation; all eyes turned to bureaucratic Brussels, aswarm with lobbyists.

If the proposal is to accept a euro embedded in a free-market Europe, with a common currency resembling the gold standard of the middle years of the nineteenth century, I would favour the adoption of the euro throughout the EU, despite possible negative consequences for the British economy. But that is not the proposal and therefore that is not my conclusion.

This essay is divided into four parts and a conclusion.

Part 1 summarises the reasons why the proposition to change currencies is being put to the British people. The shortcomings of the pro-euro position cannot be convincingly criticised unless the case for the defence is fairly put.

Chapter 1 details the alleged economic advantages of the euro which have led the British government to recommend its eventual adoption in the UK. They can be summarised as: less exchange-rate risk, lower interest rates, more trade and more foreign investment.

Chapter 2 then proceeds to recount the political advantages believed to flow from a more integrated Europe, to which the euro is seen as a notable contribution: in brief, the euro would contribute significantly to a better-functioning, more integrated, better-protected and more powerful European Union.

Before moving on to the case against Britain adopting the euro, Part 2 tries to reshape the argument by questioning three doubtful starting assumptions in both camps. One is that an active macroeconomic policy is possible, i.e. that in a sufficiently independent economy the authorities can dampen cyclical movements and keep the country on a sustained growth path with the help of monetary and fiscal instruments. The second of these assumptions is that the zone in which a currency is used must ideally be or become an optimal currency area. The third assumption is that, in the global economy of the present day, the welfare state can be saved by isolating it from outside speculation with the help of monetary sovereignty. If these starting points are wrong then both the friends and foes of imposing the euro on the British must recast their arguments.

Chapter 3 highlights the ineffectiveness of monetary and macroeconomic policies in a world of low-cost information and swift capital movements. Recent advances in economic theory suggest that the form money takes is perhaps not so important as the contenders for and against the euro have assumed: individuals on the whole will act rationally and pay attention to the real economic situation behind the monetary veil.[1]

Chapter 4 argues that the differences in structure among the economies in a currency area such as the euro zone are not as significant as the theory of optimal currency areas implies. There can never be such a thing as a currency area where monetary policy affects every individual and every business equally: forcing it to be so would be monetarily but not *economically* optimal. Rather than trying to harmonise and standardise a currency area, one should foster divergence and competition.

---

1   However fluttering this veil may be. See Yeager (1997).

Chapter 5 looks at the troubles that ail the nation-state, which seem to indicate that the meaning and importance of sovereignty, both monetary and political, may be other than assumed by either party in the euro debate. Using monetary sovereignty to isolate the country against competition is no cure for the inefficiencies of the welfare state. Creating a supra-national federation to stop people from voting with their feet and fleeing meddlesome authorities is not a defence against the effects of globalisation. Perhaps the answer to the present-day crisis of the state is to slim it down, reinforce its role as the natural constituency for democracy, strengthen it with international associations, and immerse it in the world economy. The spotlight must thus move away from currencies and policies to the economic institutional structure and the political constitutional framework within which people act.

The discussion in Part 3 tries to reach a definite conclusion on the economic consequences of a change of currency for Britain.

Chapter 6 examines the net economic drawbacks of adopting the euro. The long-term value of the euro is far from guaranteed, given the doubts surrounding the Growth and Stability Pact, the new accessions to the club, and hidden liabilities such as unfunded pensions. The effects of EMU on competition, on trade, on finance and on exchange rate volatility are not necessarily favourable and may be negative. The attempt to compensate for the lack of flexibility of the euro zone with a common monetary policy geared to the weakest economies is less than ideal for Britain. Given all this, one may ask whether the Gordon Brown tests, even if they are passed, are sufficient to settle the question of whether Britain should take up the euro.

Chapter 7 then weighs the economic arguments for and against Britain adopting the euro which are presented in Chapters 1 and 5.

Part 4 examines the political consequences of the euro. As Dr Mundell has said, a strong central state is thought by many to be a necessary condition for the success of the euro. The British government must face the constitutional questions posed by the euro. The implications of a European currency are that Britain may eventually have to give up the degree of political independence that recently allowed the government to back the USA in its fight against international terrorism. For the world in general the consolidation of the EU as a separate economic and monetary union could place an additional stumbling block in the path of free trade. Hence *Chapter 8* examines how far the euro can be expected to reinforce the trend, apparent in the proposed Constitutional Treaty, towards the EU becoming an increasingly centralised and harmonised bloc, in matters economic, political and commercial. *Chapter 9* will examine the role of monetary competition and free trade in preventing European and national authorities from abusing their powers at the expense of ordinary people. *Chapter 10* considers the political pros and cons for the UK and the EU as a whole of Britain keeping the pound.

The Conclusion will relate the issue of adopting the euro to the construction of Europe. Keeping different viable competing currencies, such as sterling or indeed the Swiss franc, within the European Union could induce central bankers to take more care of the soundness of their currencies. Variety in fiscal and economic policy usually enhances individual choice. Diversification of trade will reinforce links with the world at large. A decentralised Europe could be needed to scupper the idea of fortress Europe as a rival of the USA for global dominance. The choice of currency is a choice about the kind of Europe we wish to build: the ideas of currency competition can be translated to other areas such as regulation.

The Euro as Politics

Part 1
The Case for the Euro

The Case for the Euro

Several factors have made great currencies in the past. The list includes: size of transactions domain, stability of policy, absence of controls, fall-back value, a sense of permanence, low interest rates and a strong central state.

ROBERT A. MUNDELL, 2003

What would we say if we wanted to convince the British to adopt the euro? Such is the exercise in Part 1 of this monograph. The euro now seems to be working acceptably well. The birth of the financial euro on 1 January 1999 caused a mixed impression as the fiasco of the European Monetary System (EMS) in 1992/93 was fresh in everybody's mind. People became obsessed with the exchange rate. For a few weeks the new currency was valued above the dollar but quickly lost exchange value by more than 20 per cent. It then recovered during the US recession. The move from virtual currency to common notes and coins had little or no influence on the strength of the euro. At the end of 2003 it was at an all-time high. These ups and downs should not have been a reason to worry or exult about the currency itself, however. When monetary policies are prudent, the movements in exchange rates in the medium term tend to reflect the perception of the return to investment in the different economies.

The launching of the euro notes and coins in the first quarter of 2002 went smoothly. The logistics were well planned. The change-over may have been compulsory, but the man and woman in the street, despite some perceived price rises, did not on the whole feel that they were being given bad money for good, because the European Central Bank (ECB) was expected to aim at being as solid as the Bundesbank was over its fifty-year history. Also, the Maastricht conditions and the Stability Pact contributed to the impression of solidity, by trying to put an end to deficit financing. Since the duty for member states is to aim for a zero public deficit, there is a clear intention to keep the European Monetary Union (EMU) inflation free, or at least high-inflation free. Indeed, while the world boom of the 1990s lasted, most member states proved themselves able to run their deficits down or even show substantial budget surpluses. Even now that the public finances of a number of member states are straining under the weight of the recession, deficits are still controllable. The conservative French and the red–green German governments may be worryingly reconciled to overstepping the limit. The Portuguese at least have realised the need to rein in public expenditure. The Italians have been making efforts to reform their state pension system. But the need to avoid deficits has become, in form if not always in fact, part of the accepted behaviour of governments.

Again, it was lucky that unforeseen developments helped make the euro popular in countries of the Celtic and Mediterranean fringe of Europe, where it was feared that public opinion would find the accompanying fiscal stability too hard to bear. Spain, Ireland, Portugal and later Greece benefited from large pre-entry devaluations resulting in a decade of export-led growth; large aid funds coming from the EU also helped. But all was not due to luck. Interest rates fell to German levels because Germany put the reputation of the Deutschmark (DM) at the service of the new currency. The euro is now popular where its effects were most feared; it could also be popular in the new EU countries if the world economy picks up again. And the present Portuguese indisposition can be attributed, not to the euro, but to local macroeconomic mismanagement.

Thus the euro has had a better start than many expected

– including myself in my previous monograph for the IEA, *Back from the Brink* (1997). Though monetary union is not needed for the proper functioning of a single market, many people welcome the euro as a natural appendage to a single market and a united Europe.

If we wanted to convince the British public of the need to replace sterling with the euro, the arguments would be those outlined in Part 1.

1 THE ECONOMIC ARGUMENTS FOR THE EURO

The programme for setting up the euro stretches back to at least 1970, when a committee headed by the Prime Minister of Luxembourg, Pierre Werner, issued a report outlining the steps to create a monetary union in the European Community. That early project signalled a move away from simply seeking to establish the convertibility of world currencies to trying to create a new monetary zone coinciding with the Common Market. The project has taken some time to come to fruition but is undoubtedly having a large measure of success.

The avowed aims of monetary union for Europe are to create a solid currency that will rid Europeans of the curse of inflation, do away with national monetary borders, ease travel in a large area, free industry from a great deal of exchange risk, bolster budgetary and financial orthodoxy, and permit the comparison of prices across countries and thus foster competition and productivity in the euro zone.

The economic case for Britain giving up sterling and adopting the euro as legal tender has recently been expressed by the British government thus: 'When in 1997 the Government committed the UK to the principle of joining the single currency, the Chancellor stated that the advantages are lower transaction costs, less exchange rate volatility, more incentives for cross-border trade and investment, and potentially lower long-term interest rates.'[1]

These long-term goals, and the more particular one of easing the transition to a new monetary regime, were summed up by Chancellor Brown in his five criteria:

- convergence with the euro zone;
- flexibility of the British economy;
- effects on investment;
- continued prosperity of British financial services;
- impact on growth, stability and employment.

As an afterthought, the Treasury, in their June 2003 Study, have included trade expansion.

The stated benefits of a single currency are as follows.

1 An independent ECB, focused on price stability, will make the euro a barrier against inflation (and deflation) and will bring lower interest rates long term

According to the Maastricht Treaty (Art. 108 of the consolidated Treaty of the European Union) the European Central Bank (ECB) cannot seek or take instructions from the Council, the Commission or member states' governments, and neither can national central banks that are a part of the system, nor any individual member of their several decision-making bodies. Autonomy of the issuer of the currency together with clear rules for the conduct of monetary policy are important conditions of currency stability. Many central

---

1   Conclusion to the Assessment of the Five Economic Tests, 6.2, in *UK Membership of the Single Currency: An Assessment of the Five Economic Tests* (Cm. 5576).

banks, after they were nationalised in the years following World War II, showed themselves often ready to monetise the public debt or even finance public deficits directly by printing money; thus they became an instrument of the political cycle, increasing the money supply to bolster employment or galvanise the national economy just before an election and stabilising it just after. As the jargon phrase goes, they became 'time inconsistent'.

The need to grant the central bank autonomy in the euro zone benefited Britain, as the Labour government took advantage of this part of the Maastricht Treaty to make the Bank of England substantially free from government interference in the day-to-day management of monetary policy.

But independence is not enough. After World War I, Dr Havenstein of the German Reichsbank, exercising his power to act independently, fed the hyper-inflation with banknotes of larger and larger denominations, which he boasted he flew by aeroplane to where price rises left people without adequate means of payment. Only death removed him and opened the door to Hjalmar Schacht's reforms. Besides independence, a monetary policy rule is needed to discipline the central bank in a paper money and credit system. Hence Article 105 of the Treaty of the EU establishes price stability as the primary objective of the ECB. It is only 'without prejudice to the objective of price stability [that] the ECB shall support the general economic policies in the Community', such as 'a high level of employment'. This shows that the ECB will consider growth and employment as subordinate aims to price stability. The bank set itself the goal of keeping the increase in the Harmonised Index of Consumer Prices (HICP) between 0 and 2 per cent. True, this rule is applied only over the long run, and indeed the monetary indicator chosen by the bank, namely M3, has been expanding too speedily of late. But if we go by the criticism levelled at the ECB for not having followed the aggressive interest rate reductions of the Fed under Alan Greenspan since 2000, public opinion at least seems to feel that the ECB is showing itself to be quite serious in abiding by its self-imposed discipline. One can take it that the 2 per cent upper limit of the harmonised HICP, imposed by the ECB on itself, is really 'zero inflation', if the effects of quality improvements in the goods and services consumed are taken into account.

The costs of strong deflation are as well understood as the costs of inflation these days. In today's European economies wage stickiness is the rule, which makes a fall in final prices result in higher unemployment. In countries where resistance to corporate reform is strong (as is the case in Japan or was the case in China) falling market and asset prices are a menace for the survival of financial and non-financial companies. Hence, avoiding persistent falls in the price level becomes imperative. In May 2003 the ECB showed itself sensitive to criticism that its model did not take into consideration the deflationary pressures in parts of the euro zone by making 2 per cent inflation the aim rather than the ceiling of its policy.

The system under which the ECB functions is different from that of the Bank of England in three ways. The ECB uses a 'two pillar' strategy to assess the euro zone's inflation outlook: a 'reference value' for M3 growth rate of around 4.5 per cent and attention to a second pillar of economic data mainly on growth and employment. Second, the deliberations of the ECB are kept secret. Third, the ECB Council is answerable to no one.

This is the old Bundesbank procedure, well adapted for a time when M3 could be accurately measured because substitutes for ready money and bank credit were not generally available and when the public could not so readily store its money abroad. Measuring the quantity of money is much more complicated in today's world, when money substitutes are constantly being invented.[2] The amount of second-guessing by money managers makes secretive behaviour unsettling. Finally, a purely technocratic central bank with no democratic state behind it may not be able to withstand the cross-currents of political discontent during a slump.

The Bank of England has been very successful in its new role as an independent central banker. The three features of the new regime are: the use of inflation targeting with accurate results; a Monetary Policy Committee whose deliberations are made public a fortnight after meetings; a clear system of political answerability to democratic authorities, whereby the government sets the inflation target and the governor of the bank has to explain in a public letter to the Chancellor of the Exchequer why the target has been missed, when that is the case.

There are indications, however, that the ECB may edge towards the system of the Monetary Policy Committee of the Bank of England. Professor Paul de Grauwe, of the University of Leuwen, has criticised the use of M3 as an intermediate instrument. Several ECB watchers argue that it has effectively abandoned targeting M3. Also, demands for the ECB Council to publish minutes sooner after its meetings are increasing. If the ECB finally abandons the

---

2   The ECB aims as a final objective at price stability, which it defines as a 1.5 per cent annual growth rate of the harmonised CPI (2 per cent since May 2003). To attain that in 1999 it assigned M3 a desired annual growth rate of 4.5 per cent, assuming an increase in transactions demand for money linked to a real growth trend of 2.25 per cent year on year and a yearly decrease in money velocity of 0.75 per cent. The fact that the ECB has not managed to keep the growth of M3 reasonably near its objective should be attributed to the short time it has been operative.

Bundesbank rules in favour of something akin to the procedure of the Bank of England, after the adoption of the euro the UK would not be so exposed to volatile inflation rates.

Britain, it is true, will not benefit from EMU as much as new entrants (and old recreants). New and candidate nations stand to benefit from the expectation that they will join EMU in their own good time, as did some of the present members with less stable monetary policy records, such as Ireland, Portugal, Spain, Italy and Greece. The expectation of low inflation, the obligations of the Stability Pact, and generous Convergence Funds will set them on a steady growth path. They will not suffer sudden runs against their currency, when a transversal shock or imprudent public policies makes them lose the confidence of the financial markets. The obligations imposed by the Stability Pact will discipline their macroeconomic policy. Also, their inflation rates will in the long run converge to the average in the euro zone. The possible vagaries of such new entrants will not overly affect confidence in the euro, because the size of their economies is small in relation to those of the existing member states and their influence in the ECB Council will be negligible.

Be that as it may, the monetary policy of the ECB is based on the belief that long-run price stability is more important, indeed more achievable, than short-term counter-cyclical policy. The ECB's commitment to defending long-term price stability, rather than to furthering growth by aggressive interest rate movements, indicates a welcome degree of scepticism about the ability of central banks to manage the ebb and flow of the real economy. Hence the remit imposed on the ECB by the Treaty is well taken, and so are the upper and lower limits to the normalised HICP chosen by the ECB board.

2 Though the euro zone is not an optimal currency area, asymmetric shocks will tend to decrease in number and harshness as mutual trade increases

As Dr Mundell has shown, an optimal currency area is a harmonious area where the unified monetary policy of a single central bank will produce similar effects everywhere and hence where the central bank can with confidence apply one overall monetary policy. But since large currency areas will show structural differences among regions and industries, the question turns on the reforms that can help to reduce macroeconomic differences among regions when the region has given up the instrument of a floating currency.

But as Dr Mundell says in his submission to the Treasury, an own exchange rate is no solution to the problem of structural differences, since a principal cause of nationwide asymmetric shocks is none other than the national exchange rate: 'exchange rate volatility is the most important kind of asymmetric shock because it is truly nation specific. Such volatility or instability results in real economic changes, particularly in the real exchange rate and sometimes in the terms of trade' (Mundell, 2002: 201).

Still, real asymmetric shocks can also happen on their own, and their effects will be deeper the greater the difference in economic structure between two countries or regions. Imagine a sudden and large change in the price of an important foreign input, let us say oil. A monetary zone will react 'asymmetrically' to such a shock: the relative prices of regionally concentrated oil-intensive industries will move away from those of other regions consuming relatively less energy. A monetary policy that tries to keep prices stable on average may lead to the oil-intensive part pricing itself out of the market and to unemployment. Not letting the currency float will force the negatively affected industry to take harsh restructuring measures to bring costs in line. This kind of problem, says Mundell, also affects regions within a national state with a single currency that floats.

Given unevenness and the rigidity of the euro zone's productive structure, the euro area is clearly not an optimal currency area. Hence the Union runs the danger that asymmetric shocks will affect the different member states, accustomed to letting the rate of exchange of their national money soften the impact of such shocks, differently. If the habit of resisting redeployment of the labour force and other factors of production persists, intractable pockets of unemployment could appear, giving rise to political conflicts that would jeopardise the hard-won unity of Europe.

One of the main difficulties of the UK adopting the euro is the disharmony of its economic cycle with that of the nations on the Continent. The ECB could not adapt its monetary policy to the British cycle period. The period of British membership of the Exchange Rate Mechanism showed this.

However, in EMU, deeper economic union is helped by monetary union. The mutual influence of two elements will help alleviate the effects of a sub-optimal currency area in two ways. The first is the convergence of the economies of the euro zone thanks to growing trade in goods and services and free movement of capital among the partners. The other is the structural changes making for greater factor mobility, which member states will be forced to make by the very pressure of being in the same monetary area.

Trade is a partial substitute for factor mobility, especially labour mobility; therefore the deepening of EMU will help accommodate or reduce asymmetrical shocks. Increased trade will help bring the British cycle in line with that of continental Europe. Joining the euro is a self-healing proposition, in that being fully in EMU will increase trade with the Continent and thus expand the portion of British industry synchronised with the rest of the EU. When goods and services traded across the Channel increase from today's 49 per cent to ever larger proportions of the UK economy, this sector will necessarily move with the European cycle. [3]

There is evidence that European integration is reducing business cycle disharmony, especially if observed on a regional rather than on a country level (Wynne and Koo, 1997). These factors will not, however, reduce the importance of using all possible means to make the European economy more flexible.

A third way may open up, once the euro is fully in place and people realise that a single currency needs to be underpinned by a single political authority: the creation of federal taxes resulting in automatic fiscal stabilisers, whereby a region will carry a lighter fiscal burden when depressed, and contribute more to permanent social services when booming. But this mechanism belongs to the political side of a single currency.

3 A single currency in Europe will reduce transactions costs

Even if one can conceive of a single market with different currencies, surely things will function more smoothly with a single currency. The introduction of the euro will reduce transaction costs

---

3   There is also evidence that the so-called 'border effect', making contiguous regions separated by a political frontier observably different, is disappearing between EMU partners (Hess and Shin, 1997). Especially interesting for regional effects is Barrios and Lucio (2001).

and exchange risk, facilitate trade and capital movements, and simplify price comparisons for consumers and other purchasers of goods and services. Lower costs and more competition will boost productivity. Let us examine these benefits.

Paul de Grauwe divides the gains from the elimination of transaction costs into two kinds: direct and indirect (the latter are considered under the next heading). As far as direct savings are concerned, 'eliminating the costs of exchanging one currency into another is certainly the most visible (and the most easily quantifiable) gain from a monetary union'. He then quotes the estimate of these yearly gains by the EU Commission as between €13 billion and €20 billion, about one quarter to one half of 1 per cent of the Community GDP.[4] But those costs are attached to the use of physical notes and coins. Hence the Commission calculates that for the UK the benefits will be nearer 0.1 per cent. Moving over to the euro would then mean a yearly saving of £500 million to £1 billion. This is not an inconsiderable sum, and these calculations may be conservative.

To this we should add the non-monetary welfare gains from not having to bother with many currencies when travelling in Europe, or when dealing and trading with Europeans, something tourists, fund managers, exporters and importers will surely appreciate.

One must not, however, deduct the loss of exchange dealer revenues from this gain in transactions costs. As de Grauwe rightly says, these dealer revenues are a deadweight loss for the European economy and their vanishing only implies that the banking industry must adapt to new times.

---

4   European Community Commission (1990), as quoted by de Grauwe (2000: 58–9).

4 The single market will function better with a single currency

Indirect gains from the elimination of transactions costs come from the increase in trade and the reduction in the scope for inter-country price discrimination.

The euro will increase economic and financial integration in the Single Market and foster efficiency and competitiveness, thus creating a more prosperous Europe. Paul de Grauwe has summed up the case for monetary integration thus: 'a monetary union will have a great potential further to integrate markets in the European Union, in the same way as having the same currency, the dollar, has been of great significance for the United States in creating a single market in that country' (de Grauwe, 2000: 60–1). It is a fact that in the EU prices of similar goods are clearly more divergent between nations than within nations (see Table 1). EMU should help to bring them together.

One of the main forces for economic integration is the comparison of prices in an area where they are expressed in the same currency. Prices of goods will be more easily compared across countries; even differences in the prices of non-tradables, such as haircuts, taxi fares or train fares, will be noticeable if they are large. But this 'price comparison effect' makes its mark especially in tradables, since price differences will trigger imports of goods and offers of services. Also, the reduction of currency transactions costs will promote arbitrage and help reduce price differences between national markets.

Comparisons in wages will also change perceptions in the labour market. While employers have always compared wage costs across countries, trade unions have found it difficult to claim similar pay across national boundaries: there will now be

Table 1 **Price differences in Europe (coefficients of variation)**

	Bel	Fra	Ita	Nld	Por	Spa	All 39 cities
Video recorders	5	6	4	2	7	8	7
Printers	7	6	7	37	6	3	10
CDs	5	4	2	4	9	6	10
Perfumes	6	5	8	12	8	8	10
Tennis rackets	5	3	15	3	16	5	11
Personal stereos	12	6	10	9	8	22	12
Irons	5	3	11	2	7	2	13
Car radios	4	6	14	5	28	10	13
Sport shoes	4	6	7	5	13	8	13
Hi-fi systems	5	9	12	4	8	5	14
Radio-cassettes	12	3	20	18	19	15	15
Clothes	7	5	21	8	12	7	15
Electric razors	6	4	9	8	6	7	17
Video cameras	10	15	8	11	10	4	22
Video tapes	3	8	9	3	8	8	24
Toys	6	16	29	7	45	14	24
Headphones	20	22	39	15	42	28	27
Food mixers/processors	4	8	31	9	18	10	27
Calculators/organisers	18	9	44	8	17	40	27
Watches	10	25	27	24	38	24	38
Average	**8**	**8**	**16**	**8**	**16**	**12**	**17**

The total includes evidence from 39 cities in Austria, Belgium, France, Germany, Italy, Luxembourg, the Netherlands, Portugal, Spain, the UK, and Switzerland.
Source: HM Treasury, *EMU Study: Prices and EMU*, p. 37.

increased convergence, perhaps leading to unwelcome labour cost increases in European economies with lower labour productivity. But the introduction of a single currency will surely lead to structural reform, so that convergence need not be upwards.

An even more important effect of the introduction of the euro will be the creation of continent-wide capital markets. Though there has been movement towards single European financial markets with the freeing of capital movements, the obstacles set by national authorities are making market consolidation difficult – witness the Lamfalussy Report. Competition among markets, with the help of electronic transactions over telecommunication networks, is resulting in consolidation, especially in bond, cash and derivative markets. Hence, the first markets to cover the whole of Europe will be those of bonds (public debt and fixed interest securities), because they are much easier assets to turn into rated commodities than shares. The consequence will be a reduction of spreads and an increase of liquidity in bonds, and later more capital ready to back novel enterprises. As Dr Mundell (2002: 202) put it, 'economic convergence will be rapid in goods markets and financial assets and slow in labour markets'.

It was Adam Smith who first proposed that 'the division of labour is limited by the extent of the market'; and that money widens the market by fostering commerce and thus having virtually the same effect as a cheapening of the transport of goods (Smith, 1776: I.iii, I.iv). The euro will contribute to a noticeable increase in productivity in the EU.

When the euro is fully operational, when the Single Market functions seriously, the euro zone will be much more self-sufficient as far as macroeconomic policy and trade are concerned. The Community authorities will have the opportunity to stabilise Europe more efficiently than other areas; it may even become the growth leader of the world and replace the American economy in its role of world locomotive when the latter fails. The recent recession of 2001/02 is an object lesson in the excessive dependence of Europe on America. The new currency, its Central Bank and the Council of Economic and Finance Ministers (ECOFIN) should manage their business so as to make Europe more independent and self-sufficient if they so wish.

5 Firms will be spared the exchange risk for EU transactions

One of the most important effects of the introduction of the euro, say its defenders, is that companies will be spared continuous and unpredictable exchange rate movements with other euro zone countries which so upset business calculations. Firms should prefer a future return that is more certain to one that is less certain. Hedging for exchange rate movements is expensive. Exchange rate randomness affects the cost of supplies, export prices and marketing plans in unexpected ways. This in turn affects local investment and frightens foreign direct investment away.

Smaller member states of the EU will maintain their presence in the markets of their larger partners with great difficulty if continuously affected by movements in currency values. More generally, sudden increases or falls in prices due to appreciation or devaluation of currencies will wreak havoc in international markets and reduce the volume of trade and investment below what it could be with fixed exchange rates.

Sometimes financial markets consistently overvalue currencies for long periods, which can result in whole industries being wiped out. Such has been the case in Britain, where, under Margaret Thatcher, industry was decimated for this reason, and where today international services are virtually the only survivors after a prolonged bout of the pound overshooting its purchasing power parity (PPP).

Also, it is very difficult to conceive of a Common Market where participants could engage unilaterally in competitive devaluations (Goodhart, 1995: 477–8). Such moves would be equivalent to erecting temporary tariff barriers against imports from Union partners and could not become a habit without retaliation.

A negative consequence of keeping the pound is the instability of the exchanges. 'The whims and passions of exchange dealers, not cross-border trade, drive currencies,' notes Philippe Legrain. Any practising businessperson would want to be rid of sudden changes in the currency in which he has calculated his contracts. Sudden devaluations of the pound are a headache for British exporters, as revaluations are for importers, and, as Legrain points out, 'joining the euro would insulate half of Britain's trade from currency moves'. On the other hand, 'adopting the US dollar – as some Europhobes suggest – would protect only 16 per cent' (Legrain, 2002).

Exchange rate uncertainty affects not only trade in goods but also the exchange of services, such as those supplied by the City of London. If, instead of simply speaking of trade, one looks at the sum of British transactions on current account in and out, exchanges with EU countries come to no less than 49 per cent of the total amount. So virtually half of Britain's foreign transactions would be protected from exchange risk, whereas now, with the pound floating, all of it is exposed.

This is a material consideration for two reasons. The first is that Britain is a very open country, economically speaking. The sum total of its transactions with other countries on current account is a remarkably large one compared with its GDP, a figure equivalent to around 53 per cent of its gross product.[5] The second is that covering exchange risk with financial instruments is not as cheap or easy to do as some economists say, especially for small and medium-size companies.

Who knows what the value of the pound will be in one or five

---

5   *External Trade*, 604, March 2004, tables 2.1 and 2.2.

years? How can businesses plan properly under such uncertainty? Short of a single world currency, such as the gold standard was, the euro does offer some protection from the vagaries of fluctuating currencies.

One difficulty posed by the nature of exchange markets is that of choosing the right euro/sterling exchange rate at entry. The regrettable experience of the ERM is a warning to the British government to choose the right value for the pound when irrevocably tying it to the euro and then giving it up. The market value of sterling as E-Day approaches will not be an unambiguous marker for the rate to be chosen, for the City will typically bet on an exporters' exchange rate being chosen. The government will no doubt carefully weigh up circumstances so as to choose a rate that is neutral and does not cause an artificial boom or an unwanted slump.

The HM Treasury Study includes carefully thought-out 'Estimates of equilibrium exchange rates for sterling against the euro'. Three different methods are used to define a range wherein the accession rate should be chosen, to wit between 1.175 and 1.33 £/€. And on the ad hoc assumptions that 'the sustainable current account is zero in the UK, 3.5 per cent of GDP in the US, and the euro area has a 1 per cent surplus ... the euro sterling rate ... [would be] 1.37 £/€'. These rates are lower than they have been for quite some period in the market, a depreciation that would fill British industrialists' hearts with delight.

Whether the pound is kept or not, the euro will be used in the UK especially for financial and export transactions. Just as the Swedish krona is being shunned for the dollar and the euro by the clients of the largest banks,[6] sterling will be slowly aban-

---

6   'Swedish industries to a large extent just don't bother about the krona and keep more and more of their balance sheet in foreign currencies', according to the

doned for important valuations as EMU is increasingly successful. International businesses will try to hire their managers in euros. Exporters to the euro zone will quote their prices in euros. Pension and investment funds will reinforce the present trend of investing principally abroad and will widen their market by seeking quotation on Continental stock exchanges. Companies will try to tap euro capital by issuing euro-denominated paper. Tourists will expect to be charged in euros at restaurants and hotels. Sterling will be restricted to paying one's income tax and VAT, riding on buses and buying food, so why not go the whole hog?

6 Full EMU will increase trade

As Dr Mundell has said (2002: 197), nation-states did away with multiple currencies and with customs barriers as they consolidated an internal market: 'The basic gains from currency unification in the international sphere stem from the extension of national free trade areas to a wider unit. The larger the common currency area the greater will be the gains from trade and lending.' Such an increase in trade will stem not only from trade diversion but also from trade creation, i.e. not only from shifting sources of supply production from a lower-priced outside source to a higher-priced EU member source when internal tariff barriers become a single Common Market tariff.[7]

The effect of a currency union on trade could be large and may

---

chief executive of Svenska Handesbanken. The trend was partly caused by the 'instability' of the Swedish currency. Demand for the krona appeared to be driven by demand for Swedish equities, with the stock market 'as the last bastion of the krona'. *Financial Times*, 22 August 2001.

7   See Jacob Viner, who first made this distinction, in the Introduction to Bhagwati (1999).

have been underestimated. Rose (2000), writing for the 'Britain in Europe' group, concluded that 'one of the few undisputed benefits of joining a currency union is the encouragement of trade'.[8] The relatively low amount of trade between the UK and the rest of the EU suggests that, without the effect of exchange rate instability, it could grow to match that of its European partners.

At the present moment, Britain's trade in goods with the rest of the EU is half the total. The continuing overvaluation of sterling is surely taking its toll on British industry and on goods exports. As world trade specialist Philippe Legrain recounts, in the first half of 2002 'Britain's trade deficit swelled to £21.7bn ... Exports were 4.5 per cent down on the same period last year.' Things do not look so good for Britain either when comparisons are made with the euro zone: 'Germany's trade with the EU ... has risen from 27.2 per cent of GDP in 1998 to 32.2 per cent in 2001, and France's from 28.0 per cent to 32.2 per cent ... Britain's trade with the EU has fallen from 23.4 per cent of GDP in 1998 to 22 per cent in 2001, shaving 0.5 per cent off GDP growth' (Legrain, 2002).

A currency alignment with the euro zone and soon-to-be partners in central and eastern Europe will make trade easier with the Continent and help British industry find new markets in the EU.

HM Treasury asked Rose to revisit his paper and review his conclusions. He evaluated and combined 443 point estimates of trade increase when currency unions are formed, from 24 recent studies. The result was that only 36 of the 443 showed a negative effect of currency union on trade; most showed a large economic

---

8   Rose (2000), as quoted in HM Treasury Study, 'Submissions on EMU from lead-
     ing academics', p. 203.

Figure 1 **US investment in the EU**
US $ billion

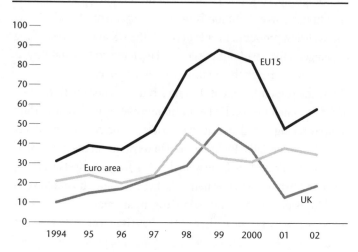

Note: Data for 1995 exclude Spain and Sweden.
Source: HM Treasury, *EMU Study: EMU and Business Sectors*, p. 61.

effect; and almost two-thirds of those estimates concluded that a currency union is associated with a doubling of trade.

Rose went further than this in his conclusions on the effect of the euro on British trade: 'My estimate is that British trade with Euroland may eventually triple as a result of British entry into EMU, conceivably resulting in a doubling of British trade and a 20 per cent boost to British GDP in the long run.'[9]

It should be mentioned that Rose's work has come in for criticism because it is not clear that there are not other forces at work leading to increasing trade when monetary union takes place.

---

9   Ibid.

Figure 2   **Japanese investment in the EU**
%

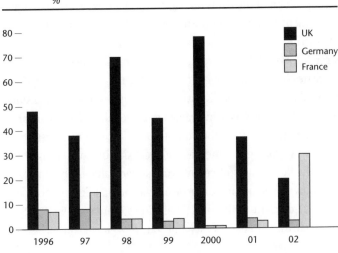

Note: Data for 2002 represents the first six months only.
Source: HM Treasury, *EMU Study: EMU and Business Sectors*, p. 61.

To the trade effect of monetary union we must add the likely increase in Foreign Direct Investment (FDI). If the pound gives way to the euro, the foreign capitalist will be more certain of the returns from his investments in the UK and will see Britain as a profitable base for selling in the whole EU.

Thus another positive effect of adopting the euro will be an increase of capital inflows into Britain, especially if foreigners see Britain as a good base for investment in the euro zone. There appears to be growing evidence that sticking to the pound is hurting Foreign Direct Investment into the UK. Japanese investment seems especially sensitive to the EMU factor (see Figures 1 and 2). Exchange rate uncertainty also affects the value of assets held by the British abroad or foreigners in Britain. Estimating the asset position of the UK is not easy, especially as regards portfolio investments; given the importance of the City as a financial centre, identifying securities issued or owned by UK residents is not straightforward. However, the Pink Book of the Office for National Statistics (ONS) attempts to estimate the net worth of the UK, so to speak: 'The value of UK assets and liabilities has doubled since 1995, with total assets being valued at £3176 billion and total liabilities at £3216 billion at the end of 2001.' Though these are stock figures, we may get some idea of their size by comparing them with the flow figures of yearly gross added value of the domestic economy: the sum total of those assets and liabilities in 2001 is a figure equivalent to five and a half times that year's GDP (ONS, 2002: ch. 8). The effect of exchange rate movements on such a sum must be huge.

7 The Growth and Stability Pact will demand zero public deficits, force further privatisation, counsel a revision of welfare entitlements, and lead to reforms in labour markets

The Maastricht Treaty demanded the fulfilment of five conditions before entry to the euro club, of which two are of continued importance for the reliability of the new currency: inflation convergence and budgetary convergence. The first is especially complicated in a monetary union, where monetary policy is exclusively in the hands of the ECB and member states can therefore not use monetary instruments to curb local inflation if their prices stray from the Community average. Then, at the behest of the German government, member states signed the Stability Pact, which indefinitely extended the obligation to keep budget deficits around zero, one year with another, or even create a surplus if the national debt was above 60 per cent of GDP. Indeed, fiscal policy is the only weapon left in the hands of the member states if they are to bring inflation down because of local overheating.

The Spanish state has gone further than most in putting this Stability Pact into effect. An organic law passed at the beginning of 2002 imposes the duty to balance the budget not only on the central treasury but also on local governments; more concretely, it forbids the fifteen autonomous regions to run deficits and to issue public debt without the permission of the finance minister, who will not grant it without previously being presented with a plan to restructure local expenditure and raise income, as the need may be.

The reason why member states are made to aim for at least a zero-deficit budgetary policy is that a common currency makes it imperative that no country free-ride on the reputation of the euro to issue excessive debt on euro terms (Goodhart, 1995: 467). The euro would lose credibility, since nobody would believe that the EU would allow a member state to go bankrupt. This is in contrast to the 'benign neglect' system of public finance in the USA, where it is not inconceivable that neither the Federal Reserve Board nor Congress would bale out a large city, as was the case with New York, or even a state in the Union, should it prove unable to honour its debts. Hence, in the EU, it is best to stop any profligate creation of public debt at source.

The aim, then, is to run at least a balanced budget during periods of moderately strong economic growth so that there is more margin of manoeuvre during periods of economic slowdown: with deficits of up to 3 per cent of GDP. If a 3 per cent maximum deficit were felt to be too harsh in times of recession, a slight softening could be contemplated. This is what Germany and France have been asking for during the low-growth period of 2001–4, perhaps frivolously to postpone overdue reforms of public pensions, state health services and restricted labour markets. There may be some merit in the British policy of a long-term financial framework for public finance, aiming at a surplus in boom times and allowing temporary deficits in leaner years. But the spirit of the Growth and Stability Pact must be kept if the euro is to accumulate a good reputation.

Now, a zero-deficit policy need not imply reducing government spending, but it at least keeps its growth in line with that of GDP. In times of low growth it is an added incentive to the privatisation of nationalised companies. It also demands a second look at ever-growing social security, health and pension benefits. Since social contributions usually take the form of a tax on wages, financing a cash-hungry welfare state drives a wedge between what employers disburse and what employees get in their pay packet. This leads to employers substituting capital and machinery for labour, and employees showing less willingness to work, and brings about a higher than normal unemployment rate or a smaller working population, or both. The euro Growth and Stability Pact will force member states in the euro zone to rebalance their welfare and health systems and follow the Dutch and British example of fully capitalised private pensions.

The Danish and the Swedish 'No' to the euro were precisely based on fears that a single currency would lead to cuts in welfare and social services. The clash between the Italian prime minister and the unions shows that any move to change labour laws so as to make the economy better able to resist increased competition would be totally impossible if there were no euro to steel the government's resolve. The euro is seen as a menace by many on the left of the political spectrum, but employers defend it precisely because it teaches backward-looking organisations the free facts of life.

In sum, the credibility of the euro demands a zero-deficit fiscal policy or something approaching it. If a country shows a higher inflation rate than average or a wider temporary deficit than prudent, ECOFIN and the Eurogroup within it will watch over its fiscal policy, to ensure that it comes back in line. This will surely impel member states to privatise, revise welfare entitlements and reform labour laws.

True, the Stability Pact suffered a hitch in 2003 owing to the refusal of France and Germany to bring their budget deficit below a figure equivalent to 3 per cent of GDP. The ECOFIN committee has refrained from fining these two member states, thus throwing into some doubt the commitment to balanced budgets. Perhaps this is an indication that the pact is too rigid in not fully taking into account the difficulties posed to public accounts by economic downturns, and that an arrangement along British lines should be substituted for it: that government debt be kept below 40 per cent of GDP over the cycle and that a budget deficit be run only to finance investment.

Owing to its good management of public finances, Britain will become a force for structural market reform on the Continent if it adopts the euro. The European project treads a delicate path between American capitalism and old-style socialism. Europhobes deplore the policies defended on the Continent, especially by the French under every political dispensation. France seems always to look backwards: the imposition of a thirty-five-hour week, the out-

and-out defence of the CAP, the refusal to privatise Électricité de France and the French national railways, the perpetual rhetoric of anti-Americanism, the outmoded defence of budget deficits – all are in danger of infecting the whole of the EU unless Britain leads a countervailing force from the inside. This countervailing role for Britain is almost impossible if it doesn't adopt the euro, especially because ECOFIN is losing importance in relation to the Eurogroup, the ad hoc meetings of the euro zone ministers.[10]

It is only natural that macroeconomic debates in the EU should focus on the euro: budget deficits, exchange rate policy, tax harmonisation, convergence of financial rules and regulations, the single financial market and labour market policy are only a few of the questions impinging on the smooth functioning of the single currency.

If Britain wishes to impress on Continental nations and the European Commission itself the need to find a third way between unbridled capitalism and a dirigiste economy, in order not to find that that the EU is an increasingly uncomfortable dwelling, giving up the pound for the euro is mandatory.

---

10 The British government first heard with alarm from the head of Britain's permanent representation in Brussels that they were not invited to discuss the measures to be taken when Germany and Portugal looked likely to flout the deficit obligations of the Stability Pact. Currently Britain is not invited to discuss any matters in the Eurogroup, an increasingly important informal forum consisting of 22 ministers and top-level finance ministry officials. British efforts to be included back in 1997 failed. The Eurogroup president also on occasion organises a press conference, after its meeting but before the ECOFIN meeting, thus announcing some important decisions prior to consulting the British.

8 However, the size of the euro monetary zone and the strength of the ECB will ensure the survival of the 'European socio-economic model' in a globalised world

The harshness of the Stability Pact should not lead one to think that Europe is going to return to Manchester capitalism. It may instil some degree of prudence in the conduct of public affairs but the size of the euro monetary zone and the strength of the ECB will also ensure the survival of the 'European socio-economic model' in a globalised world.

As was mentioned above, the use of the euro as a unit of account will make wages more comparable across the euro zone and reduce the amount of unfair wage competition, thus reinforcing the European model of considerate capitalism, a model that makes for social integration and peace. The statutes of the ECB give it sway over monetary policy, but not over exchange rate policy, which the Treaty has left in the hands of the Council of Ministers, which can agree with the ECB a softening of the euro exchange rate to allow for a softer approach to globalisation. Such a course of action would not have been open to smaller euro zone member states with currencies subject to unsettling international speculation. But a large monetary zone with a world currency can be a little less Darwinian. In a way, the creation of the ECB could be thought of as the setting up of a cartel of central banks that could stray temporarily from the straight and narrow if needed without running the danger of an EMS-type crisis. All this is good news for the moderate left, who could not abide by a strictly capitalist model for Europe.

9 The euro will soon become a world currency and thus will be a source of seignorage for the EU

The use of the euro to denominate, settle and finance large amounts of international trade and services will of itself make it an international currency. But if the euro turns out to be a safe currency as well, then it will be widely used as a reserve asset by central banks, financial institutions and private citizens, both in and outside the euro zone.

The seignorage (see Box 1) expected to be obtained in 2002 by the ECB was €13 billion per year, roughly equivalent to the new banknotes yearly put in circulation by the different central banks in the euro zone. There were problems in the sharing of this seignorage among the member states, and it was agreed just in time, before the physical euro started circulating, that the several national central banks would partake in the ECB seignorage according to their GDP and the size of their population. The amount of seignorage will increase as use of the euro in the world spreads day by day.

The fact that Britain is not in the euro zone, however, reduces the appeal of the euro as a reserve currency. The central bank of China, for example, is known to be averse to keeping euros for as long as the existence of sterling indicates a lack of confidence in the new currency by one of the EU partners.

The remit of the ECB, the size of the euro zone and the growing popularity of the euro not exclusively in the area where it is legal tender guarantee that the European currency will soon be able to look the dollar and the yen in the eye.

Box 1 **Seignorage or the gains from issuing money**

'Seignorage' is a form of government income. It is so called because it used to be what the *seigneur* (the king, or the authority of the merchant republic) charged for coining and stamping the precious metals brought to the mint by private people. Seignorage was charged over and above the cost of thus assaying and processing the gold or silver (a cost called 'brassage' from *bras,* meaning 'arm' in French), as a clear gain for the service of guaranteeing the purity and weight of the coins. The value of this service was often abused by the kings debasing the money.

The wide use of its currency increased the income of the state in two ways:

- the seignorage obtained by the yearly minting of coins;
- the inflation tax obtained by debasing or re-stamping those coins;

    – minus the physical cost of minting or that of bringing in and restamping the coin.

Also, in so far as denominating public debt in a readily accepted and safe metallic currency increased the willingness of the public to hold it, a quasi-seignorage was reaped by the government in placing a larger quantity of debt with no discount.

With fiat money, commercial banking, electronic accounting and a liquid market for government bonds, the ability of governments (through their central banks) to reap nominal seignorage has become larger, as:

- the material from which coins are made is less expensive than gold and silver;
- the denomination of notes can be as large as the central bank wishes with the same production cost as for small denominations;
- the cost of maintaining the commercial banks' cash base electronically at the central bank is infinitesimal;
- the standardisation of virtual bond markets widens the market for, and reduces the cost of, public debt.

But the multiplication of outside money (coins plus notes plus commercial banks' deposits at the central bank), and of government debt beyond what individuals and businesses and commercial banks wish to hold, causes the public to flee the currency, pushes prices up and shortens bonds, with two effects:

- a reduction of the real value of the seignorage and quasi-seignorage through inflation;
- an increase in the interest rate spread of bonds over the return of safer assets.

Hence, there is an optimum amount of nominal seignorage to be obtained and of public debt to be placed, given the inflation and shorting caused by excess money creation and bond issue (White 1999: ch. 7). That optimal amount can be larger the wider the use of the currency worldwide and the more liquid the market for government debt denominated in that currency.

As Mundell (2000) notes, 'when money is overvalued [it

is] a fiscal resource of the first magnitude'. The yearly gross seignorage the ECB will achieve is reckoned to be equivalent to the €13bn in new notes it will put into circulation every year plus the cash balances of commercial banks with the System of European Central Banks. To this sum should be added a 2.5% inflation tax on a note circulation of some €300bn, amounting to €7.5bn yearly. The seignorage will of course increase *pari passu* with the entry of Britain and other member states, and the use of the euro worldwide. The gains from the lower spread and more liquid market of government bonds for countries previously using unstable money will be considerable.

2 THE POLITICAL ARGUMENTS FOR THE EURO

In his essay on monetary unions (1995: 452), Goodhart asks: 'Why do currency questions have such political resonance?' The political arguments for the creation of the euro are never clearly spelt out, least of all by a British government that does not want the constitutional dimensions of replacing the pound with the euro to be aired in public. Politics is not as easily amenable as economics to sober analysis. We will try, however, to classify the arguments advanced in favour of the euro for its beneficial political consequences, cutting out much of the rhetoric.

The most important political argument for the UK making the euro its currency can be put by rephrasing Dean Acheson's dictum: Britain lost an empire half a century ago and has still not found a role. Fully throwing in its lot with Europe, it is argued, is the most sensible and realistic policy.

Other political gains for Britain if it joins EMU are:

- The British monarch's portrait will stay on the euro coins and thus will be a powerful symbol for the role that the UK can play in Europe and the world.
- Giving up the pound is a signal that the British renounce armed conflict against their EU partners for ever, as the ability to print money in an emergency has always been a weapon of war.

- By adopting the euro Britain will at last pull its due weight in the Community. If the British reject the euro, they will reinforce the 'perfidious Albion' prejudice. It is a deeply held belief in the euro zone countries that the UK is always dragging its feet in matters European, or even that it is a Trojan horse for the USA. The gesture of finally adopting the euro will allay all misgivings. Britain will then be able to disagree with its European partners without anybody harbouring suspicions of disloyalty.
- The EU model of capitalism has a fairer chance of surviving if all nations of Europe join forces to make it a success. Tony Blair's New Labour policies do not stand a chance of being accepted on the Continent unless Britain is seen as a full member of the EU club. Many baneful ideological forces are at work in Europe and even old-style socialism might raise its ugly head again.
- The logic of the euro makes for the reinforcement of the common European institutions, a development that will not necessarily lead to a federal state if Britain is fully present at the writing of the constitution.
- With Britain fully in, the EU has the weight to exercise a moderating influence on our American friends, and at the same time can help to keep transatlantic ties strong.

These points can be generalised so that the political desirability of the euro as a single currency can be seen as a strong force of unity.

1 The euro will be a powerful symbol of European unity

One of the avowed defects of the EU is that its denizens are weakly pro-European. If anything, local and national sentiment seem to be on the increase. Disillusionment with the EU is rife, compounded as it is with anti-globalisation attitudes.

Traditionally the coinage has been one of the privileges of the monarchy, symbolising its power and the unity of the land in which it was legal tender. The new currency has come to represent the new togetherness of Europeans, flowing from the free agreement of proud and ancient nations. The circle of stars that appears on the coins and notes of the euro is now part of the daily lives of 300 million people, who up to now were united only by a passport cover and obscure commands issued from remote Brussels. The euro will make people in the EU proud to belong together.

2 By pooling seignorage, EU nations are demonstrating that they do not envisage having to wage war against each other

The monopoly of the issue of legal-tender money has traditionally been a reserve weapon of war, since issuing money is a speedy way of financing war when other means are not at hand.

The Common Market was founded on the undertaking that France and Germany would never fight each other again. It is therefore not too far-fetched to say that the euro was founded with a similar expectation among all member states. As Goodhart notes, 'If the nations of Western Europe no longer expect to wage wars among themselves, they no longer need national instruments of wartime finance. Moving to a single EC currency therefore represents both an actual and a symbolic renunciation of any

Box 2 **Currency boards**

Pegging one's currency to another standard, be that the gold standard or the dollar, implies imposing a very strict discipline on the central bank.

In effect the central bank promises to exchange on demand a fixed amount of gold or dollars for a fixed quantity of the national currency and vice versa. Thus the Bank of Hong Kong hands out one US dollar for every HK$7.50 proffered it and HK$7.50 for each US dollar. To keep this promise the bank must have in its vaults or on call the same amount in US dollars as the value of the HK$ held by the public.

The central bank becomes simply a till for automatically exchanging the local currency for the standard. The monetary policy of the country now fully depends on that of the Federal Reserve, for the amount of the local high-powered money cannot increase unless the Fed expands the amount of dollars it issues.

The state cannot incur debts that cannot be readily financed by its tax intake or generally raise its expenditures above what is covered by taxes, because the market will doubt that the central bank will not in the end accommodate the government by printing local money. This is how the Argentine currency board came to grief. Whatever the amounts lent by the IMF or the temporary exchange control measures taken by the government, there will be a run on the central bank reserves unless it has enough dollars to answer every call.

The implicit rules of a currency board forbidding public deficit finance and private credit bubbles are parallel to the rules of the Maastricht Treaty and the Stability Pact. The difference is that the currency board can be evaded for a time and then lash in without warning, while the vigilance of the ECB board and of ECOFIN is continual.

One of the advantages of setting up a currency board over straight 'dollarising' is that the country keeps the seignorage on its base money (cash plus banknotes plus the reserves of the banking sector at the central bank). A disadvantage is that the local currency may be exposed to runs if the authorities do not abide by the rules (as happened

anticipated need to finance the protection of national, as opposed to EC sovereignty' (Goodhart, 1995: 455).

By acting as an antidote against narrow nationalism, and by stopping one of the main means of war finance, the euro consolidates peace on the European continent.

3 A single currency and a common Central Bank will give rise to less friction than a 'serpent' or a system of currency boards linked to the DM

There had been suggestions that the DM could have become the money of Europe, since it had spontaneously become the main reference for all other currencies. However, by giving up the DM and merging it in the euro, the Germans have accepted and the French have welcomed this reining in of possibly excessive German power. This will reduce occasions of tension among European nations. Again, joining EMU and adopting the euro are surprisingly less drastic steps than establishing a currency board. On the surface there seems to be no more extreme way of renouncing monetary sovereignty than totally giving up your national currency. The main alternative is a 'currency board', anchoring the national currency to a safe standard (see Box 2). But a country under such a regime surrenders monetary policy totally to the issuer of the standard to which the national money is pegged. Joining EMU and adopting the euro avoid the automatism of a currency board, since participating member states will have a say in the monetary policy of the euro zone. All national central banks are represented on the ECB board and representations on behalf of the economies of each member state will be heard and taken into account before decisions are reached on interest rate policy. The Argentinian situation is extreme, but one can see what anti-foreigner sentiments can erupt when a harsh monetary policy is imposed from New York without warning and without recourse on an unsuspecting citizenry.

Another great source of political conflict in the 1930s was the use of beggar-my-neighbour devaluations to export unemployment to other countries. This is now impossible for member states in the euro zone, and indeed will encourage harmonisation of macroeconomic policies, much to the benefit of everyone in times of recession.

4 The euro will make the citizens of the different member states accept measures that would be 'politically impossible' without the authority of the Union

The euro plays the role of a self-denying ordinance, or a constitutional rule forbidding measures that are time inconsistent. It will allow governments to be more responsible in resisting demands for short-term benefits that are paid for dearly in the long term. By joining EMU, countries have undertaken to respect the Stability Pact, which enjoins them to aim at zero-deficit budgets. If governments act irresponsibly they are open to a reprimand or even a fine from the Commission. Even more effective is the appeal to the European sentiments of the voters when public policies go astray: the former Spanish prime minister, Señor Aznar, or the Portuguese prime minister, Senhor Durão Barroso, would not have dared take the harsh measures their countries needed if they were not in EMU.

5 Europe is trying to define a distinctive Third Way in social and economic matters

The political economy of the euro zone is neither old-style socialist nor neo-liberal. EMU will make it possible to combine monetary orthodoxy with a broader government remit in social policy than is the case in the USA. Europeans must accept globalisation but, it is argued, they must tame it and control it, so as to put economic forces and transnational companies at the service of man and community. Having a common currency will help create a space where this more humane society can flourish with the help of the positive forces of capitalism.

Small countries with local currencies are not able to resist the pressures of international speculators when they think a government is being soft in its social policies. A large monetary zone is not beholden to the whims and fears of international markets and has some leeway for correcting mistakes in one or two of its regions without facing financial run.

6 The convergence of the fiscal and economic policies of the member states necessitated by the euro will slowly reinforce the cohesion of the EU

The euro will make it imperative to set up a European Federal Union with a democratic constitution. The theory of optimal currency areas shows that they cannot function unless there is an automatic system of fiscal transfers. The small tax income of the EU, capped at 1.27 per cent of the Union's GDP, is a brake on the movement towards a united Europe. Fiscal transfers and automatic fiscal stabilisers would help the euro monetary area function smoothly. This could soften resistance to moving some tax powers from member states to the Community.

More generally, the euro demands a wholly new fiscal regime throughout Europe. The various member states have given up their monetary sovereignty and can fight local inflation or recessions only with budgetary measures. Also, the welfare state that characterises the EU ethos must now be financed by taxes and not by hidden or overt deficits. Hence an effort should be made towards fiscal convergence and against unfair fiscal competition by some small member states. Widespread tax evasion and avoidance undermine the use of fiscal instruments to complement and soften the effects of EMU.

With a single money and a single central bank it will be imperative that the Union as a whole follows a common macroeconomic policy. ECOFIN will grow into the crucial role of managing the business cycle of the Union.

7 A single currency in the end demands a single political authority

The history of previous monetary unions shows that a single currency cannot last unless underpinned by a central authority with fiscal (and perhaps other economic) powers. This implies some degree of political union. As Wim F. V. Vanthoor concludes in a book analysing the history of European monetary unions since 1848:

> The most important lesson was that monetary union is only sustainable and irreversible if it is embodied in a political union, in which competences beyond the monetary sphere are also transferred to a supranational body. In this respect, the Maastricht Treaty provides insufficient guarantees, as budgetary policy as well as other kinds of policy (price and wage and social policy) remain the province of the national governments. (Vanthoor, 1996: 133)

In a later study of the lessons of history for EMU, Bordo and Jonung (2000) are in a contrarian way forthright in their conclusion about the political prerequisites of EMU. 'A precondition for the EMU to succeed and be stable in the future is that the individual members of the EMU display forever a similar commitment to their common goal as did the advanced nations to the gold standard rule more than a century ago. This is a major challenge facing EMU. It is unclear how well it will succeed in creating such a convergence in policy preferences in the future' (Bordo and Jonung, 2000: 38).

The comparison with the gold standard is not quite exact. The rule requiring adherence to gold was not a political commitment but a belief in the necessity of obeying the laws of nature, so to speak. It lasted only forty years, up to 1914. It was beset with incidents and runs, and disappeared as a multi-country order under the assault of war. But the comparison helps make the point that an ever stronger commitment will be needed if the euro is to withstand the test of time, as the dollar has for nearly a century and a half. The very difficulties that a single currency poses for inelastic European economies will make it clear that a central authority is needed to impose harmonisation and thus lead Europe towards becoming an optimal currency area. And if the importance of having one's own currency when there are 'military threats to vital interests' is taken into consideration, the new currency can become permanent only if it is the instrument of a political union, as Walter Eltis quite reasonably argues.[1]

Another reason why the euro will be a ship without an anchor if it dispenses with political moorings is that there is a limit to the acceptance of central bank independence in a democracy. The legitimacy of a central bank, be it independent or not, grows from the acceptance of its decisions by the people, especially in times of crisis. A central bank without a democratic mandate will have difficulty in weathering hard times: hence, the need for a political authority to sustain the euro. The connection between the euro and the creation of a European federal state is well understood by the creators and backers of the new currency on the Continent, even if the details of the political organisation that will result in the end are not known. The creation of the euro will prove decisive in the creation of a united Europe.

1   In his comment on the Bordo and Jonung paper. See Eltis (2000: 55–6).

8 The euro will reinforce the perception that Europe is becoming one of the world's major power blocs

Europe should not only be able to hold its own with the USA and emerging Asian powers in economic matters but should also have its own voice in political questions. The end of the cold war propelled the USA into the role of sole great power. But other centres of power may be forming in the Far East, and the present American monopoly cannot last for ever. It is only prudent that there should be a Europe aiming to take on the role that Britain played in the nineteenth century, holding the balance of power vis-à-vis the other great nations in the world.

This should not result in a break-up of the EU's special relationship with the USA. The fate of the free world depends on that friendship. The US government may make mistakes in playing the role of worldwide sheriff, however, or may decide to seek isolation behind a wall of sophisticated weapons. It may even try to form a Union of the Americas, from which European interests could be excluded. In any of these cases it would be a relief if the EU grew to be a second world power with enough economic, commercial and military resources to counterbalance any unwise moves on the part of the USA.

9 World peace will have a greater chance with a stronger EU

Not only will power be more evenly shared with the Americans but also the free market and free world trade will have a greater chance of being fully adopted by the EU. With Britain not trusted by its partners, efforts to launch a new trade round within the WTO could be jeopardised.

Part 2
Monetary Sovereignty

The very politicians and economists who repudiate Keynesian policy at home become fervent Keynesians when they contemplate the horrors of British membership of the single currency.

ROBERT SKIDELSKY, 2002

Before turning to the question of whether Britain should keep sterling, we should examine what we know about the nature of money and about the functions and future capacities of the nation-state. Though it may be true that changing one's monetary standard has deep implications for national sovereignty, one should first give some thought to the reduced role of money and to the limits of state power in a modern open economy. There could be a need to recast the arguments both for and against adopting the euro.

Thus, as regards the ability to influence the real economy with monetary instruments, the friends of the euro predict that economic convergence brought about by the single currency will help the ECB govern the European economy with a Continent-wide monetary policy; and the friends of sterling hold that it will be much easier to manage economic fluctuations by means of the Bank of England interest rate. Thus also, as regards the consequences of globalisation on nation-states, the defenders of EMU hold that the nation-state is obsolete and impotent, while the defenders of national sovereignty, especially in Denmark and Sweden, fear the discipline of the euro for its effect on the welfare state. But one's views may change in more ways than one after seeing the limited effects of monetary policy on the real economy in a globalised world, be it applied by the ECB or by the Bank of England. The same may happen to one's political hopes for Europe or Britain after realising that the nation-state has been enfeebled, not so much by its small geographical size, as by the excessive span of its functions.

It is my contention that the notion of sovereignty is stretched and misapplied as regards the economic and political consequences, both favourable and unfavourable, of adopting the new European currency. It is as if both camps started from an unspoken Keynesian assumption that monetary and political authorities can exercise discretionary influence on society if their territory is of the requisite size.

For Keynes, the capitalist system could not function properly without continuous intervention by politicians and civil servants; and what is more, he thought that unelected officials could be trusted to work for the public good. The defenders of the euro, pointing to the fact that national currencies are too small for an independent macroeconomic policy and ruing the time when national central bankers enjoyed monopoly powers, extol the advantages of a single European central bank, able to pursue monetary stability while governments pursue active macroeconomic and welfare policies. Surprisingly, many critics of the euro also want an active monetary and social policy, but think it should be put into effect within a sovereign national state.

Now, *what if* ...

- a successful anti-cyclical policy is not within the reach of a central bank;
- central banks cannot directly and permanently contribute to full employment by expanding the money supply or reducing interest rates in the money market;
- central banks turn out to be unable to change the real interest rate on long-term credit;
- the real rate of exchange cannot be managed in a discretionary manner;

• the welfare state should turn out to be unsustainable whatever the size, national or continental, of the area over which it reaches?

Then, a whole family of economic and political arguments *for and against* the euro lose relevance.

One may ask those in favour of the euro why they want to impose a new currency if people will increasingly be able to choose whatever money suits them best. Equally one may say to those wishing to retain monetary sovereignty that there is little point in wanting to control monetary policy, or wield the instrument of a national central bank interest rate, or intervene in foreign exchange markets, as economies become increasingly globalised. The discussion should turn on whether the various economies are flexible and open enough to ride over monetary disturbances and what political institutions will contribute to making them so.

Assume for a moment that in trying to exercise sovereignty both national and European authorities cause more harm than good. In that case there is room for different types of monetary and political arrangements, allowing Europe to reap the benefits of currency competition untrammelled by attempts to manage the economy. And the monetary policy should operate in the environment of a minimal state, freeing Europe from the attempt to regulate everything under the sun.

The battle for and against the euro must then be fought on another field. The choices would be those of centralisation versus individual choice, and of government discretion versus competition among institutions and jurisdictions. To join or not to join is not a question of sovereignty.

3 DOES MONEY MATTER?

Economists have always had great difficulty in integrating money in their models of the economy. If the analytical framework is that of a perfectly competitive economy, tending towards a state of general equilibrium, what is the point of perfectly informed transactors keeping liquid money in their pockets? From that point of view money is but a veil that should be pulled aside to get at the real phenomena. If, on the other hand, the starting assumption is that cash balances are needed because transactors are immersed in a world of uncertainty, is not the belief that the authorities can manipulate money to counter fluctuations and make the economy grow a return to the belief in Plato's philosopher kings?

Money is two-edged

Explanations of the need for money go back at least to Aristotle. Everyone is familiar with the three functions of money: measure of value, means of exchange and store of value. All three are of great importance in helping supersede the primitive barter economy and moving to one where people can sell without buying (and vice versa) and not have to take what they do not want. The store of value function is especially useful in allowing individuals to deal with uncertainty: receipts may unexpectedly not tally with payments, so that a store of cash comes in handy. Notice that the value stored in coins or notes is simply one way of dealing with the uncertainties of the future: credit is the supply of a store of value by a saver to a borrower. Hence, this third function summarises all the financial services of a community that help multiply productivity. Adam Smith (1776: II.ii) saw this very clearly when he defined money as capital – that is to say, as a factor of production.

However, this useful instrument of trade and credit is not the coins, notes, book entries or electronic digits that we perceive with our senses, but the permanent value symbolised by the monetary instrument. Smith saw this too: 'When, by any particular sum of money, we mean not only to express the amount of metal pieces of which it is composed, but to include in its signification some obscure reference to the goods which can be had in exchange for them, the wealth or revenue which it in this case denotes, is equal ... to the money's worth more properly than to the money' (II.ii.17). So that individuals, if they can help it, will not be taken in by the appearance of money, but will use the real value behind its nominal worth. That is to say, people will always discount the nominal money they receive by its purchasing power in the market.

The first way in which money matters is the positive one of allowing people to transact, because they accept it as a representation of real wealth; and a greater ease of transaction helps create greater wealth.

For individuals, the mental operation of calculating the real value or purchasing power of nominal money is not a simple one. Gathering the necessary information is not always easy. The result depends on the goods and services in which each individual intends to trade. There are short cuts but the result is always approximate: consumer price indices, prices at the factory gate, the GDP deflator, the rate of exchange with a world currency are some of the many used. But one must not forget that strictly speaking each person should use his own price index to calculate the value of the nominal money he uses. It takes time before people realise that a central bank is misbehaving by over-printing or under-issuing money.

Another reason why it is possible to deceive ordinary people into making them use worthless money is the fact that the issuing of nominal or fiat money is always an oligopoly. Setting up a currency network is not like opening a restaurant. Money is a 'network' good, in the sense that the more people use it the more useful it becomes. People will be resistant to changing the currency they normally use for another that may not be accepted so readily. Hence, incumbent issuing banks are protected by an entry barrier. This means that the issuer may be tempted to inflate and debase its currency. When legal-tender laws impose the use of a national currency and exchange controls are set up as an exit barrier for captive residents, this natural oligopoly is transformed into an even more dangerous monopoly.

Despite all these barriers to entry of competitors and to exit of users, ordinary people can still protect themselves by taking account in their contracts of the expected debasement. If the rate of inflation is steady year in, year out, transactors will discount it easily. Entrepreneurs, workers and producers will not think that an increase in the prices they obtain for their goods and services is due to an increase in their relative prices, so they will produce and consume as much as before despite the fact that they are richer in fiat money. Contracts will be adjusted to take account of this constant rate of inflation. Nothing changes, and an aggressive monetary policy becomes futile.

To overcome these defensive moves the issuing monopolist will try to surprise the public so that they cannot readily calculate the real value of money. To bring about temporary money illusion extra money will suddenly be created, thus misleading the public into imagining a sudden burst of real prosperity; and then, just as suddenly, a correction will be imposed in the name of responsibility. This will eventually have the effect of reducing the demand for money and financial services and also of making the supply of these services more expensive as banks have to charge insurance interest over the real cost of lending. It will also make contracting more complicated and bring about random distributional changes.

The second way in which money matters is a negative one: the currency may be abused by the issuer to charge an inflation tax, which cannot be obtained unless the authorities randomly deceive the users of their currency. This upsets expectations with the end result of reducing growth.

In sum, real money and credit are inherently good because they are a factor of production; and nominal money can be a force for bad if it is strategically managed.

Money is neutral in the long run …

This lurid tale of central banker misbehaviour need not be taken as a faithful representation of reality in all circumstances. But even when monetary authorities are well intentioned, the sceptical conclusions of what is called 'inter-temporal' or 'rational expectations' macroeconomics still apply: see Box 3.

Let us imagine that the central bank takes measures aimed at pulling the economy out of a recession, such as lowering short-term interest rates or expanding the monetary base. Can we count on them to be effective? If private agents were inert pawns in the hands of authorities they might react like Pavlov's dogs to cheaper, more abundant money and invest or consume more than before. However, people are not content with viewing policy measures as once-and-for-all acts of God. They see these measures as moments in a behavioural continuum, where future circumstances and expected policy measures weigh on present situations. It may be the case that the public interprets a monetary expansion as the sign of a parlous underlying economic situation and will not be induced to invest or to spend, either because they think more monetary easing is on the way on the part of the authorities, or because the present reaction of the central bank suggests that the economy is going to deteriorate and they would be well advised to save more. This seems to have happened in Japan during the last ten years.

As Milton Friedman (1976) noted when criticising Keynesian economics, the injection of liquidity will certainly cause an expansion of *money* national output (i.e. real output multiplied by the price level), but it is impossible to tell how much of that expansion will be represented by new real activity and how much by price increases. It may be the case in the short run that the injection will revive real production, if at first private agents cannot tell an inflationary rise in prices from an increase in the prices they can charge for their output; but in the long run, they will not be taken in by a mere monetary phenomenon, since rational people react to real incentives.

Friedman himself noted another consequence of the classical view that expectations make an active and discretionary policy nugatory. It is real, not monetary, incentives which count in

Box 3 **Rational expectations and the currency***

If we assume that people make use of all the information in the market relevant to their personal decisions and that they will learn from their mistakes, then it is safe to conclude that monetary policy can no longer be conceived as a game the authorities play for their own ends with inert agents as pawns.

The discretionary measures of monetary authorities cannot be conceived as once-and-for-all decisions, as giving rise to no future unwanted counteracting individual reactions. Central bank measures will affect the future decisions of other agents because these agents form expectations about the future behaviour of the authorities: they study the current decisions of the authorities and discount future behaviour. Private agents will react differently depending on whether the current monetary measure was anticipated or not and on whether they believed it to be transitory or permanent in character.

Rational expectations is an equilibrium concept used to model dynamic economies where there is self-reference. Models of such economies must take account of the fact that expectations shape the future values of variables used by agents. They must also take account of the fact that those agents will have a better knowledge of the structure of the economy in their sector than any outside observer. Hence, as Muth posited, forecasts made by the economist who has the model will be no better than forecasts made by agents within the model.** Another way of putting this is to say that no outside authority can know better than the market.

Models taking as given that equilibrium will be reached

because people act rationally (in the sense that they form expectations about the future that turn out to be true) are counter-intuitive. This theory can be interpreted heuristically, however, in the following way. Agents that act outside rational expectations will, in the words of N. E. Savin, eventually notice that they are making systematic mistakes and will try to revise their forecasts. 'Agents are not in equilibrium until they have learned to form rational expectations' (Savin, 1987: 79d).

Rational expectations theory carries fatal consequences for active monetary policy. These dynamic self-reference models generate recurrent but aperiodic business cycles that are not due to erroneous, readily improved perceptions by agents. Governments cannot smooth cycles. There is also a connection with the incurable error in Phillips curves, since active inflationary policies will not permanently deflect the labour market from its 'natural' unemployment equilibrium (the Lucas critique of econometric policy evaluation procedures – see Lucas, 1976).

Only fully anticipated and permanent policy rules can create a permanent framework for rational behaviour by individuals. The question of how to impose this kind of behaviour on monetary authorities is crucial in the discussion of the euro. The builders of the EU prefer explicit rules guaranteed by treaty. A more realistic solution may be monetary competition.

* I have used Febrero (1998) in writing this summary.
** Muth (1961), as quoted by Sargent (1987: 76c).

the end; and an effective policy (or at least one capable of being evaluated and recommended) must base itself on creating permanent expectations. Hence one should aim at putting rules-based policy regimes in place.[1] One of the luminaries of 'rational expectations macroeconomics', Professor Lucas has disparaged the idea that monetary authorities can influence economic performance for the good by taking discretionary measures to influence aggregate behaviour.[2]

In sum, the long tradition that money is neutral and can only impinge on the real economy for the worse if central bankers act strategically and discretionally has been taken up again with renewed force by the 'inter-temporal' or 'expectations' school of macroeconomics (Lucas, 1972).

But if in the long run money, when well managed, is neutral, why worry about adopting or not adopting the euro? As long as the ECB behaves properly and supplies a reliable currency, there would be no loss in giving up sterling for the euro.

… but there can be money illusion in the short run

If Friedman proposed to fix the increase of base money at a constant rate, come what may, it was obviously because

---

1   Friedman (1959) proposed that base money creation should be put on a permanent growth path parallel to the real growth rate.

2   Lucas (1980). Professor Paul de Grauwe, whose textbook (2000) is set in the mould of neo-Keynesian economics, still seems to believe in an activist central bank as an engine of growth. In a recent article, he attributed the growth record of the USA to easy money and the fiscal deficit and decried the exclusive fixation of the ECB with inflation: 'central banking is not just about keeping inflation below 2 per cent', he wrote in the *Financial Times* (Grauwe 2004).

he expected the real economy to become capable of accommodating shocks with quick changes in relative prices. If real interest rates and real factor prices, especially wages, respond immediately to changed conditions, there will be no need to rely on monetary pump-priming to counteract prolonged recessions and their consequent long-term unemployment. This is how the gold standard worked in nineteenth-century Britain. Come a financial downturn, the pound sterling would stay pegged to gold, a monetary steadfastness barely relieved by a reduction in the bank rate; wages and the labour force would be quickly and drastically cut; numerous bankruptcies would be declared; and barely a year would pass before the recovery was under way.

Conditions today are very different from the gold standard period, though some economies, especially those of the USA and the UK, are less rigid than others. As Mancur Olson recently pointed out, it was an achievement of Maynard Keynes and John Hicks to point to sticky wages, among other sticky prices, as the culprits in the twentieth-century saga of long periods of unemployment.[3] After remarking that sticky wages as an explanation of unemployment was rather ad hoc in Keynes's model, Olson suggested that in many democracies cartels, unions and lobbies contributed to making wages and many prices rigid: as far as wages were concerned unionised workers had an interest in keeping competitors unemployed, through minimum wage legislation and other ploys; and large employers of labour also

---

3   Olson (1982: ch. 7). Keynes rightly pointed out that forcing a wage reduction to cure involuntary unemployment was no solution by itself: the reason for long recessions is not the *level* of wages but the lack of *variability* of relative wages over time.

had an interest in keeping the wages of non-unionised workers low by means of a large reserve army of the unemployed (Olson, 1982: ch. 7, p. viii).

4 THE VAIN CHASE AFTER CURRENCY AREA OPTIMALITY

The belief that money matters a great deal in modern economies comes in two different forms. One is that the liquidity services of a stable currency are indispensable in a capitalist economy and that therefore inflation, especially unstable inflation, reduces growth. The other is that money can be managed at will so as to counteract the cycle and maintain full employment. I have just argued that, while accepting the need for today's issuers of fiat money to keep the credit system on an even keel, the belief in the powers of discretionary monetary policy to deliver growth and employment is, in the long run, an illusion.

Mundell's argument for EMU

One of the forms that this monetary illusion takes is in the theory of optimum currency areas. This is the idea that the central bank of a monetary area can manage the currency optimally when the different regions of this area have attained convergence in their business cycles, their industrial structures and their standards of living. As Ronald I. McKinnon put it (1963: 717), managing the currency optimally here means that the government, with the central bank, by wielding fiscal and monetary tools and a freely flexible exchange rate, can attain 'three (sometimes conflicting) objectives: (1) the maintenance of full employment; (2) the maintenance of balanced international payments; (3) the maintenance of a stable internal average price level'.

This concept of an optimal currency area was proposed by Robert Mundell, the winner of the 1999 Nobel prize for economics. In an almost unnoticed article (Mundell, 1961) he laid the ground for the imposing edifice of the euro: in no more than nine pages he set out some necessary conditions for European EMU to function 'hitchlessly', as Schumpeter would have said.

In his paper, Mundell argued explicitly against freely floating exchange rates and implicitly for monetary unions: this has been his consistent position up to the present day, when he has taken the role of foremost champion of EMU and the euro.[1] He put forward the idea that a country could not maintain full employment while correcting its external deficit by means of devaluations of its currency, if the country had, like Canada, a very diverse regional structure. Under those conditions, one either had a different floating currency for each region, or one tried to steer the variegated regions of that economy towards convergence in cycle, structure and living standards. This latter solution was clearly preferable, since it permitted the creation of currencies accepted over large areas (and ideally throughout the world): people want their currency to be liquid with wide acceptance and ease of disposal. As an afterthought, Mundell noted that a non-optimal currency area could approach optimality if its productive factors were mobile between industries

---

1   'Exchange rate volatility is the most important kind of asymmetric shock because it is truly nation specific. Such volatility or instability results in real economic changes, particularly in the real exchange rate and sometimes in the terms of trade' Mundell (2002: 201).

and regions. As he put it, 'an essential ingredient of a common currency, or a single currency area, is a high degree of factor mobility' (ibid.: 661).

Here we can see the origin of two ideas current in the euro zone today – and present in the Chancellor's five conditions. One is that all efforts should be made to attain economic convergence among the different countries of the EU. Another is that, since factor mobility, especially labour mobility, is patently lacking in the EU, the imposition of the euro over divergent European regions will, within reason, prove an irresistible force for reform and for greater economic flexibility.

But a *monetary* optimum (for central bankers) need not be an *economic* optimum (for ordinary people). National economies are made up of countless individuals and firms, each with their own structure and each affected differently by the monetary policy of the central bank. Bank credit and stock exchanges may move in sympathy with the local cycle and thus affect large groups in a collective fashion. But each business is otherwise differently affected by changes in monetary policy and short-term interest rates; indeed, each faces different interest rates depending on its credit-worthiness and expectations. There will never be a monetary policy adapted to the circumstances of each and every economic actor in an area. Apart from trying to avoid unnecessary financial collapses of the kind suffered in 1929–32, central banks are there to maintain the value and liquidity of the currency, not to steer the aggregate economy.

Greater factor mobility in the euro zone should not be treasured because it makes life easier for central bankers but because it is in itself a contribution to growth. Such factor mobility will be quickened by the very fact that the area is *not* an optimal monetary zone. In itself structural divergence is an incentive for trade, cross-country investment and productive migration. Structural convergence of member states, if brought about by EU funds and not by competition and learning by doing, puts a brake on growth.

It will of course be easier for a central bank to apply the strict measures needed to protect the value of money if the population of the country is accustomed to its presence and policies. The USA is not an optimal currency area, despite internal migration and federal fiscal stabilisers: the different regions go through their own peculiar slumps and booms that work as incentives for change. After ninety years of the Federal Reserve system, Americans accept its rulings even if they do not suit all regions and businesses equally.

The attempt to turn Europe into an optimal currency area could lead all euro zone states to be equally rigid and synchronous, and we would find ourselves with an optimal currency area and a pessimal economy.

It is often felt that the more rigid an economy the greater the need for monetary sovereignty to alleviate economic downturns. But one should not conclude from this that managing the currency acts like a magic wand to overcome the problems of economic rigidity. Variable inflation may alleviate temporary pain but it reduces the capacity of economies to grow in a sustained manner. The sensible conclusion should rather be that central banks maintain a stable monetary regime and governments remove barriers to internal and international competition.

Let us suppose that a monetary area such as the euro zone suffers a shock (for example, one like the oil crises of the 1970s). The monetary area will function optimally if either its economic structure is uniform and all shocks affect all regions symmetrically or if, though some of those regions have economic structures that make them suffer asymmetrically from the shock, factors move rapidly from places and industries affected to those unaffected. Mundell's model thus points the EU in two directions if it wants to have a single currency: either it forces all parts of the euro zone to converge to uniformity, or it pushes through reforms that make all parts flexible, especially in the labour market.

Two important mechanisms of a globalised economy are missing in Mundell's model, however: the increasing proportion of international trade in world GDP; and the fast-growing supply of financial services at an ever-decreasing cost. Regions in crisis will not need devaluation so badly if they see their foreign markets grow spontaneously and if they can finance the shortfall in their foreign accounts for a more extended period, while they correct their cost structure.

The optimal currency area is losing importance with the growing globalisation of the world economy. To function well the EU does not need business cycles to converge, nor taxes to be harmonised, nor labour markets to be submitted to identical regulation across the euro zone. Europe needs only stable currencies, free financial flows and trade open to the whole world.

An optimal currency area is an oxymoron, a perpetually receding horizon that should never be longed for. The more flexible and open an economy, the more liquid and accepted its currency, the less the need to join a monetary cartel such as EMU.

Splitting the dollar?

One of the conclusions of the optimal currency area model is that 'the optimum currency area is not the world ... The optimum currency area is the region' (ibid.: 659, 660). Should one then have different floating currencies for homogeneous regions across borders? Should one have different state 'dollars' in a non-optimal currency area, such as the USA?

This question is often turned against defenders of currency competition rather than against backers of the defective optimal currency area model. It should really worry the latter. Why should the region be optimal as a currency area? The firms and industries of an area can never be of the same size, number and cost structure. So, by *reductio ad absurdum*, the optimal currency area is the individual firm. Alternatively, infinite factor mobility is not a given in any region, however small it may be. Factor mobility is good per se, and if currency sub-optimality spurs a country towards greater flexibility (as the gold standard used to do), all the better. The optimal currency area model is empty.

Since the crucial elements of a monetary regime are common use of the currency and stability of its value, the appropriate attitude when confronting monetary change is prudent conservatism. It is one thing to create new currencies or join them into a monetary union when stability is missing. It is quite another to make experiments when the need is not overwhelming.

The argument against currency competition which is derived from observing the unity of the dollar area is less than convincing when one looks at the track record of the Federal Reserve System. During the 'great contraction', as Friedman and Schwartz called it (1963: ch. 7), the system failed dismally, and did so for the whole of the USA and indirectly for the whole world. Throughout the slump the New York Fed saw the need to take measures to save solvent banks from liquidity crises and to sustain the banking system by open market purchases.

A large majority of the Federal Reserve governors opposed such measures, however.[2] It is at least conceivable that the worst accident in the history of capitalism could have been avoided if there had been more than one dollar standard and issuer in the USA in 1929–32.

Neither has the track record of the single dollar been outstanding in later years. I am referring not to the ups and downs of the exchange rate but to the irresponsible alternations of tight and loose monetary policies, as during the Vietnam War, the Volcker period and the Greenspan years.

When monetary policy matters

Frequently, to try to compensate for lack of price and wage flexibility, economies pursue policies of devaluation against other currencies, or money injections by the central bank, or automatic fiscal stabilisers based on the possibility of running budget deficits.

In today's socially rigid economies, creating short-term money illusion sometimes seems to be the only way to soften economic fluctuations. The welfare state has made individuals increasingly intolerant of uncertainty and sudden change. An inflationary policy helps prop up sectors of the economy for a time while fundamentals reassert themselves again. The more transient result of active monetary policies is stock exchange elation, as share prices reflect temporarily improved company results. Private consumption may stay up for some time longer. Low interest rates and

---

2   Friedman and Schwartz (1963: 306, 311, 363–4; also section 7 of ch. 7, 'Why was monetary policy so inept?').

cheap mortgage policies mean that the housing market is more robust. The hope is that the economy will be ready to start again on a sounder basis when the inflationary illusion wears off.

Experience has shown us that inflation must not be allowed to run out of control. The central bank must be able, in our highly rigid societies, to use short-term interest rates to 'cool' the economy when its own previous monetary easing has overheated it. But however nimble the central bank, monetary sovereignty in today's moral-hazard atmosphere is Hobson's choice: inflation, take it or leave it.

5 DEMOCRACY AND THE NATION-STATE

Much of the argument around the adoption of the euro turns on the alleged obsolescence of the nation-state. The single currency is inevitable, some say, because the nation-state is too weak to control and direct as much as it tries. The single currency is to be feared, say others, because it will be the death knell of the welfare state. Both are in a way right but exaggerate their case.

The globalisation of the economy and society, the openness of the world economy and the new facilities for cheap travel and ready information are undoubtedly reducing the control of the state over its citizens. The answer of centralisers is to create cartels of nation-states and of central banks, so that their writ runs over a larger zone from which individuals and firms cannot so easily escape. The answer of the nationalists is to try to maintain monetary sovereignty, so as to avoid having to trim their welfare systems. Perhaps the answer is to slim the nation-state down and reinforce its role as the natural constituency for democracy. Jurisdictional competition in and among states could turn out to be a better way of defending individual freedom and maintaining world stability than super-state consolidation and centralisation.

From warfare state to welfare state[1]

The coining of money used to be one of the essential appurtenances of sovereignty: now many countries around the world are happy to dollarise their economies and twelve historic nations on the continent of Europe have given up their currencies for a new, untried money. In the past, not only was seignorage essential to governments as a source of revenue, but inflation itself, though often unnecessarily abused in peacetime, was seen as an essential weapon in wartime, given the inertia of money users who continue to transact in a currency even while it is being depreciated.

This willingness to give up the national currency may be an indication of a wider crisis in the institution of the state, which often seems incapable of encompassing defence, the economy, business, health, welfare, culture, entertainment and other dimensions that in many countries it used to control. The growing unpopularity of military power is not the only force that seems to be undermining the modern state. The globalisation of human affairs due to reductions in transportation and information costs, increased international trade and cross-border services and expanding population movements have all reduced the ability of nation-states in isolation to supply public goods or reduce public 'bads' – that is, deal with the diffused consequences of the activities of people who do not receive the returns, or pay for the costs, of their actions. To many it seems obvious that states should be superseded by international institutions or merged into larger federations to internalise, so to speak, those external effects that escape the control of individual states. The question is whether the one public good that

---

1   Ferguson (2001: 98–106) coins the phrase 'from warfare to welfare' to characterise the growth of the 'servile state'.

only nation-states and smaller jurisdictions seem able to deliver, namely democratic control and participation by the people, will be lost in the effort to create larger and allegedly more efficient political entities.

Nation-states took a long time to become the main characters on the stage of domestic politics and international relations. They were born in Renaissance Europe, among the remnants of feudal Christendom. Organisations that resembled the modern state had existed in other lands but only China had in common with Europe that peculiar institution, a strong structure of civil servants.

The states of Europe experienced a first aborted take-off in the sixteenth century when matrimonial alliances resulted in ephemeral confederations of kingdoms and lordships under one sovereign – the prime example being the Spanish empire. They were the first vehicles for the absolute power of kings and queens lording over matters civil and ecclesiastical. These confederations suffered a crisis in the first half of the seventeenth century in the form of the loss of the Netherlands and Portugal by Spain, the Civil Wars in England, the Fronde in France, and the Thirty Years War in Germany. Then the apt use of science and technology, commerce and finance allowed a select few states, Britain, France and Prussia, to grow strong in the eighteenth century. States underwent a surprising transformation in the nineteenth century: they slowly became the guarantors of the law and order needed for commerce and finance to flourish, and saw their powers almost reduced to the bare minimum needed as a framework for a peaceful civil society and for the growth and diffusion of wealth. Though nationalism and mass politics, the portent of things to come, appeared on the world stage by way of the French Revolution, the rout of Napoleon conjured for almost a century the temptation to use state power for world domination.

From 1815 to 1870, the spontaneous order of free economies was allowed to continue on its way. Then the power of the state multiplied by capitalism was hijacked by nationalist leaders adept at playing power politics. They harnessed democratic mass politics to strengthen the apparatus of the state. To obtain the loyalty of the masses, Bismarck first struck on the idea of granting social benefits, so that disaffected socialist workers should come to rely on the state for their most peremptory needs, a Machiavellian move soon imitated in other states. In the steps of Bismarck, governments lorded over industry and trade and imposed social norms through state education and often state religion. For three-quarters of a century nationalism, democracy, welfare and military might grew together (Lindsey, 2002). Now that the dreadful consequences of totalitarian nationalism have become clear to the inhabitants of the civilised world, almost the only relic of state expansion seems to be a bloated welfare system. But this relic is far from harmless and may end with the state acting as an enlightened slave owner on a scientifically cultivated plantation (Jasay, 1985: 274–82). (See Table 2.)

The resistance of taxpayers to paying for an ever-increasing public expenditure to maintain today's bloated state is expressed not only through the ballot box but also by their voting with their feet and moving into the black economy or taking their money to fiscal havens. The instinctive reaction of governments with a stake in growing public expenditure is to try to create a cartel of nation-states under the form of a European Union, where taxes converge (upwards) and the limit on EU revenue is finally lifted.

Some people who feel defenceless without the protection of a

Table 2 **From warfare to welfare**

Government finance in the UK	Percentages	
	1898	1998
Gross public expenditure per cent GDP	6.5	39
Defence per cent of public expenditure	36	7
Debt service	21	9
Civil government	20	n.d.
Education	10*	12
Social security	–	30
Health	–	17
*Revenue****		
Excise duties	29	16***
Customs duties	19	0.5
Income tax	15	26
Death duties	13	1
National Insurance contributions	–	16

* In 1898 includes Art and Science.

** Items are percentages of total revenue.

*** In 1998 includes VAT.

Source: Ferguson (2001: 105).

paternalist state jump from observing the spontaneous interna-
tionalisation of the economy to demanding the construction of
super-states to carry out the tasks of impotent nations.

Multi-state constructions, such as the European Union, are
two-sided: by creating larger markets they multiply the possi-
bilities for individuals to escape the embrace of bureaucracy;
but by building larger and more inclusive institutions they give
civil servants a larger and more defensible territory over which
to work. Many believe that only super-states and international
organisations can fill the void of nation-states undermined by
the economic and social activities of individuals spread around
the world. Some of those who defend a single money, backed
by a harmonised fiscal system, and sustained by a single federal

government, apparently feel the need to restore an all-encompassing government: and since this cannot be national, so let it be European.

Central banks and governments

At first, different institutions performed each of the two functions that characterise central banks: the management of the state debt and the management of forms of money other than coinage. The first establishment for non-metallic currency management was the Banco della Piazza di Rialto (1587), and for debt management the Banco del Giro (1619), both in the merchant republic of Venice. The Bank of Amsterdam (founded in 1609) was born to carry out the same functions as the Banco di Rialto, but soon made a market for stocks and shares in the local exchange, where the public debt of the Holland province was traded. The Bank of England, from the moment of its foundation in 1694, fused the two functions. It was granted the London banknote monopoly in exchange for becoming the government banker (Ferguson, 2001: 113–14). After that most central banks followed the same pattern, except the Federal Reserve, set up in 1914: it was established to unify paper money and provide a remedy to banking crises with 'an elastic currency' (Friedman and Schwartz, 1963: 189–93); only later did it come to manage Treasury paper and the national debt.

Poor performance of the currency management function, in part due to the pressure of mountainous national debts created to finance World Wars I and II, led to most central banks being taken over by their governments. That move proved disastrous for the value of currencies: never had rates of inflation been higher than under state central banks.

The return to stable money has been brought about not through the privatisation of the state central banks but through granting them independence from their political masters, sometimes coupled with a duty to obey rules and reach pre-set goals. It is understandable that many an economist shows scepticism when confronted with this new dispensation and demands the added guarantee of free capital movements and currency competition (Ferguson, 2001: 163–8).

The venue for democracy

There is one essential contribution of the modern state that supranational institutions are unable to supply: the nation-state is the indispensable home for liberal democracy. Westerners have learnt that mass democracy cannot work for the well-being of the individual unless it is tempered by the rule of law and the division of power. They also know that civilised institutions cannot endure unless they have the backing of the sovereign people. Hence the nation-state, properly fenced, is the venue for the exercise of democracy and freedom.

The UN and other international organisations such as the EU and its parliament are parodies of the modern democratic state. With all its faults, the nation-state, when it is not in the grip of tribal fundamentalists, is still the least bad vehicle for the expression of the will of the citizens.

Maybe the solution to the shortcomings of the modern state is not to merge it in grander organisations but to reduce it to the essential functions that make it indispensable. These are defence, law and order, an independent judiciary, the guarantee of individual rights, the preservation of property and enforcement of contracts: all the functions that are necessary for the exercise of individual and political freedoms. There will be a need for agreements with other friendly states to complete that part of these necessary functions which cannot be performed on a national basis, but international cooperation should not take the form of cartels of old monopolists to stop individuals from voting with their feet. Mere legal rules to bind politicians and voters are unequal to the task of paring down the state. Monetary competition, world free trade and free capital movement may still do the trick.

Part 3
The *Economic* Case for Keeping Sterling

We are in danger of assigning to monetary policy a larger role than it can perform, in danger of asking it to accomplish things that it cannot achieve and, as a result, in danger of preventing it from making the contribution that it is capable of making.

MILTON FRIEDMAN, 1967

After first presenting a strong case for full economic and monetary union in Europe, Britain included, we must turn to the question of whether it is in the interests of Britain and indeed of Europe as a whole that sterling should disappear and the euro become the one and only currency of all the countries of the EU. We can do so with greater confidence now that we know the limits of current monetary and political ideas so often bandied about in the discussion.

The different aspects of the question are not easy to separate. The economics turn on:

- the reliability of the single currency;
- the size of transactions costs when running two currencies in a single market;
- whether it is important to hit upon the 'right' value for the pound when joining the euro zone;
- whether monetary union eliminates exchange risk between partners;
- the effects of monetary union on competition, trade, investment and employment;
- the conditions for an efficient European capital market;
- whether a single monetary policy is appropriate for countries with different structures and cycles.

Then there are institutional questions that relate to economic aspects of the cases for and against joining the euro:

- the need for a Stability and Growth Pact enjoining zero public deficits;
- the likelihood of labour market reforms to make European economies more flexible;
- the ability of member states to fund or transform their pension and health systems to avoid financial disaster.

We then look at these economic issues in the context of the Chancellor of the Exchequer's five tests.

In considering the economic issues, one should distinguish between, on the one hand, keeping the euro once it has been adopted or newly adopting it if monetary stability was lacking in the past; and, on the other, giving up a sound and established national currency for no very sound reason. On whichever side of this dilemma a country finds itself, it should never be forgotten that reforming the economy to make it more adaptable and efficient may be more important than the currency one uses; and joining a monetary zone that under-performs may be a sure recipe for imprudent monetary policies.

I would not give the euro up as a Spaniard, and perhaps not if I were a Frenchman or a German, for the discipline it imposes on traditionally profligate treasuries. The effects of joining the euro for Spain and Ireland have been positive, though perhaps temporary: true, they are remote from the heart of the euro zone, and the monetary policy of the ECB has paid attention mainly to conditions in central Europe and has allowed inflation to be higher in both those economies than it would have been with well-behaved domestic central banks. But in the longer term these countries seem to have profited from giving up their currencies for one almost as well trusted as the DM.

Strictly speaking the UK is part of EMU, the Economic and Monetary Union of Europe, in so far as it participates in stage two of the EMU project but not stage three, the single currency. But with Sweden and Denmark it has not 'yet' joined the euro zone. The British prime minister has declared himself in favour of Britain joining at some point. Some may be restive at the time he is taking to start the campaign for the 'Yes' side. He has defined the path the government will follow to win over an unconvinced public at the promised referendum, however. He rests his argument on the political inevitability and the long-term economic advantages of replacing the pound with the euro, but will suspend the move until the short-term dangers to the British economy from such a step have lost their potency. As for Chancellor Brown, he has summarised the economic advantages as being lower transactions costs, less exchange rate volatility, more incentives for cross-border trade and investment, and potentially lower long-term interest rates. The possible economic disadvantages he believes temporary and tractable, and he has summarised them under five suspensive conditions. The results of the first review of these five conditions in June 2003, based on a thorough study by HM Treasury (2003),[1] is that at the moment only one is entirely fulfilled, namely the impact on financial services, and two are close to being fulfilled. The exercise will be repeated in 2004.

---

1   HM Treasury, *UK Membership of the Single Currency: an Assessment of the Five Economic Tests*. Cm 5776 (June 2003). And another 18 studies.

6 THE ECONOMIC EFFECTS FOR BRITAIN OF FULL EMU

The discussion of monetary sovereignty in Part 2 leads directly to the following starting point for the economic discussion: as Buiter and Grafe put it (2003), 'for the UK, whether to join or not to join EMU is, from a strictly economic point of view, not a life or death question'. This may sound surprising, given the heat of the discussion about the euro and the likelihood of recurring short-run costs when giving up monetary sovereignty. But when an economy is as acceptably managed as that of Britain those hitches could be overcome with some difficulty but not too much delay.

The temporary losses from fully joining EMU should be more than compensated by net permanent gains in the longer term. If the balance of economic advantage is not very large, however, or not even clearly positive, then the change would be worth the economic cost only if the new political European order implicit in EMU was clearly favourable to individual freedom and effective democracy. The deciding factor is whether the united Europe being built by Brussels on the Continent is that of an open society based on a respect for free markets and private property and on citizen power. This makes the hidden political agenda of EMU the paramount question.

Purely economic reasons for keeping sterling

1 Institutional competition between the ECB and the Bank of England

As Robert Mundell pointed out (1960), monetary policy is penned within an iron triangle; only two of the following three conditions can be attained: free capital movements, an autonomous monetary policy and a stable exchange rate. Britain has chosen the first two, as has the EU as a whole.

In modern welfare states monetary policy does have repercussions on the real economy in the short and medium term, so it is imperative that central bankers do not behave imprudently. The goal of prudent monetary policy has been addressed with different types of policy frameworks: central bank independence; monetary policy rules; and, the least discussed, institutional competition.

Independence of central banks from the political process is now a generally accepted system in Western nations. The bank must not receive instructions from governments and it must not be implicitly beholden to the macroeconomic or financial policies of the government by being assigned a full employment goal or by being forced to lend funds to the government or act as its bankers. The Federal Reserve is independent of presidential instructions, except that the chairman is appointed by the President for a fixed term. The Bank of Japan also decides its own policy, but the prime minister chooses the governor. The Bank of England Monetary Policy Committee is self-governing too, though the government sets the inflation target and the governor has to explain to the Chancellor publicly when it fails to meet this target. The ECB is totally free of any institutional or political ties and cannot lend to the EC or the member states. While central bank independence is becoming well established, the relationship of monetary authorities to popular sovereignty is less well organised. Here a growing trend is to impose on central banks a monetary rule, or at least to force them to make it explicit. This is still not the case with the Federal Reserve, which enjoys an open legal mandate and follows a monetary strategy policy whose final objectives are confusedly specified, and the Bank of Japan, nominally independent but susceptible to political prompting.

In Europe, however, both the Bank of England and the ECB have to follow explicit monetary policy rules. The Bank of England, in contrast to the Federal Reserve, has its inflation target set yearly by the Chancellor of the Exchequer. The Bank of England's Monetary Policy Committee meets monthly and decides changes in short-term interest rates by simple majority. Information about the inflationary expectations of the MPC are transmitted to the market by publishing the minutes of its meeting with a short time lag. Members of the MPC are held individually responsible for their votes if the Chancellor's inflation target is not met. Dissent is encouraged with a margin of only one vote sometimes occurring.

The ECB follows a monetary policy regime in the tradition of the Bundesbank. It also has an obligation primarily to maintain the purchasing power of its currency and only secondarily to back the economic policies of ECOFIN when its monetary objective is achieved. But the ECB determines for itself what the permissible variation in consumer prices is (at present from 0 to 2 per cent). And it does not target inflation directly but up to recently has used M3 (liquid funds in the hands of the public) as an instrumental variable. There is doubt that, with the fashionable fixation on *stable prices*, either institution is committed enough to *stable money*: there are situations when a fall in prices does not break the

Box 4 Taylor rules, output gaps and technological shocks

Managing a fiat or paper money financial system undergoing perpetual change and innovation is much more complicated than was administering a central bank under the gold standard. Taylor rules are used to model the actual behaviour of central bankers and prescribe their policies.

Taylor rules are observed regularities of behaviour of central banks when trying to maintain the value of money with the instruments of market intervention at their disposal. These regularities of behaviour are modelled with the help of algebraic expressions. These expressions formulate high-powered-money suppliers' 'reaction functions' to data observed in a given monetary zone.

There is a whole family of Taylor rules. The simplest form of reaction function was formulated originally by J. B. Taylor in 1993.

$$i_{nom,t} = (i^*_{r,t} + \Pi^e_{t+1}) + g_1 (\Pi_t - \Pi^*) + g_2 (\breve{Y}_{r,t} - \breve{Y}_t)$$

Here the dependent variable is the short-run nominal interest rate [$i_{nom,t}$] that the bank fixes from time to time. To explain this rate the following arguments are included: the unobservable equilibrium real interest rate of the economy [$i^*_{r,t}$]; the inflation expected in the next quarter [Π^e_{t+1}]; the current rate of inflation in so far as it is higher or lower than the bank's inflation objective [$(\Pi_t - \Pi^*)$]; and the 'output gap' of the economy – that is to say, the difference between the actual rate of growth and the long-term non-inflationary output trend [$(\breve{Y}_{r,t} - \breve{Y}_t)$]. Ideally the money interest rate set by the central bank must be equal to the real equilibrium rate plus the expected inflation rate $[(i^*_{r,t} + \Pi^e_{t+1})]$. But the bank would be expected to set it higher if the current inflation rate was above the inflation objective of the bank, and the rate of growth of output was above the equilibrium path. Usually the inflation gap and the output gap are weighted equally $[g_1 = g_2]$.*

From being a model of the observed behaviour of a central bank for the use of Fed watchers and other speculators, Taylor rules soon became prescriptions as to how the bank *should* behave in an inflation over- or under-run, or an output over- or under-run. If used to prescribe the conduct of monetary policy, Taylor rules can become dangerous. The equilibrium interest rate of the economy will suffer an upward shift when productivity increases owing to a technological shock, because the demand for capital will rise, but that shift may go unnoticed and monetary policy may turn out to have been too permissive. The output gap surely is an unreliable predictor of deflation, since in periods of stagflation a large output gap may appear at the same time as rising prices. Finally it is difficult to tell acceptable falls in the price level due to technological shocks from unacceptable deflation due to a negative demand shock.

In sum, prescriptive Taylor rules may often turn out to be defective. Central bankers must select the relevant variables. They must weight money inflation and real growth properly when assigning values to the *g* coefficients. They must remember that their policies can influence the real economy only in the short run and will often have chaotic effects.

Given the shortcomings of the various Taylor rules

used by central bankers, as well as their less than foolproof governance rules, it is dangerous to concentrate all monetary power in a single pair of hands. Only competition among central banks can be expected to weed out defective money management.

* Summary based on Castañeda (2003: 115 *et passim*).

stable money rule, namely when productivity increases reduce the price level without a deflationary effect.

The ideal framework for central bankers in a world of fiat money with no anchor is still a matter for controversy. There have been many attempts to model central bank behaviour, in the guise of a whole family of 'Taylor rules', as they are called. These models are controversial in their details and their effects (see Box 4).

In a more empirical mode, there is much to be commended in the governance system of the Bank of England, so much so that Gordon Brown has promised to seek reform of the mode of operation of the ECB before Britain joins. Whether he will succeed is doubtful, though there is a growing number of people from the member states in the euro zone who also like the approach of the Bank of England or the Riksbank, with more flexible inflation targeting. In any case there seems to be no valid reason for Britain imposing upon itself a second-best system, just because the government wants to join a euro zone full of restrictions, thus making the best unattainable.

The logical conclusion to the absence of a certain recipe for good monetary management is to rely on institutional competition among central banks with no exchange controls and no legal tender laws. The way out from the blind alley of confused allegiances and imperfect rules is that currencies should be compared one with another by investors and markets.

If we assume that central banks try to maximise the seignorage they obtain from people using their currency, then competition among money issuers can be effective in imposing discipline. The costs of issuing paper money and indeed electronic money are quite low compared with the face value of the notes or computer entries that represent it. Central banks are leaders of clubs of commercial banks that use currency because they want to base the money they in turn issue to clients on a safe base. The more the currency is demanded by the public, the greater the seignorage earned by all. Consequently, central bankers will be very sensitive to commercial banks and their clients starting to use another currency.

Unlike commercial users, the general public may react slowly to the debasement of the currency they are accustomed to using, since money is, as we have remarked, a network good with a high cost for those who turn to another issuer. But currency competition need only affect marginal financial transactors to be effective.

If what we want is *stable money* we must not rest content with rules and regulations imposed on monetary committees. We need the long-stop of competition to ensure that consistent transgressors will suffer a reduction in the demand for their currency and a fall in their seignorage earnings. Other things (which we will consider presently) being equal, one of the strongest arguments for keeping sterling (and the Swiss franc) is that it makes the ECB face institutional competition.

2 The transactions costs of keeping two currencies

Calculating the reduction in transactions costs from substituting the euro for sterling is usually one-sided. As Professor Minford has explained in the Treasury Study, one has to compare the present value of the savings in currency dealers' margins and in tourist inconvenience with the costs of changeover to the euro (Minford, 2002b: 176).

An EU Commission study of 1990 calculated that the average saving on exchange commissions would be around 0.4 per cent of GDP. Minford notes quite rightly that this figure would be lower for the UK, which has a more advanced banking system than most of the other member states, a saving of 0.1 per cent of GDP being realistic. To understand this one must distinguish between commissions charged and the use of resources. Commissions, if they are not in payment of opportunity costs, are pure transfers, which must not enter into our calculations. Only deals in notes and coins use up significant resources. The additional cost borne for foreign exchange transactions in a computerised system is near zero, so that inter-banking, inter-company and credit card currency deals are virtually costless, whatever the margins charged on them. A figure of 0.1 per cent of UK GDP is £1 billion at present-day prices: it will be a decreasing amount in real terms because of technical progress. With a 4 per cent discount rate, that saving has a present value of £25 billion. On the other hand, the one-off cost of substituting euros for pounds, from coins to vending machines to accounting systems, was calculated by a House of Commons committee at £30 billion, rather more than the capitalised value of the annual gain, unless we add the gain in convenience from a single currency for tourists and business travellers (Minford, 2002a: 23–4). So the net gain from lower transaction costs would be roughly zero.

3 The exchange rate at entry

The experience of choosing the 'wrong' sterling/DM exchange rate when joining the Exchange Rate Mechanism (ERM) has left a deep scar on the British consciousness. Another scarring experience was the merger between the Ostmark (OM) and the DM after the Berlin Wall fell: Chancellor Kohl chose a one-for-one rate for pensions and a two-for-one rate for other transactions, when the black-market rate was around seven for one. In the British case the mistake of 'shadowing' the ERM, before formal entry, caused a surge in inflation, and this was followed by a sharp contraction when formal entry was at too high a rate. In the German case East German industry was priced out of markets.

A closer look at these instances lightens the blame in the British case and deepens it in the German. Once-and-for-all price rises, though unwelcome, may have been the British economy's mechanism for adapting to a monetary devaluation; the harmful outpricing of East German production may have been the effect of labour and enterprise rigidity.

In the Treasury Study Buiter and Grafe (2003: 32) quipped that 'we are all Keynesians now or the nominal exchange rate would be a matter of indifference'. They backed up this remark by distinguishing the 'wrong' money exchange rate at which Ireland and Germany were locked into the euro and the speed at which the real exchange rate moved back to what one can take as equilibrium.

It is generally agreed that Ireland (and Spain) joined EMU in 1999 at an undervalued rate. 'The resulting boom in real economic activity and in asset prices gradually eroded this competitive advantage. In a common currency area this is precisely the way market forces are supposed to bring about an adjustment in international competitiveness. It is effective and need not be associated with asset bubbles and crashes' (ibid.).

Germany, as many believe, joined both the ERM and the euro at an overvalued rate. Using three deflators to estimate the equilibrium rate from the money rate, unit labour costs, the CPI and the GDP deflator, they perceived two phenomena. One was the higher speed of correction from 1995 to 1998, when the DM floated partially under the ERM, as compared with 1999 to 2002, after locking the DM irrevocably to other euro currencies. The other was the effectiveness of adaptation even from 1999 to 2002. The slowest variable to respond was unit labour costs, as one would expect in the German case.

This means that real exchange rate changes are not to be gainsaid by interventions in the money rate, not even by irrevocably fixing the rate. It also means that when exchange rates are fixed the economic mechanism is less nimble, especially in rigid Continental countries. The real exchange rate can fluctuate for the wrong reasons, such as imprudent conduct on the part of central banks, as has been the case in Mexico and Argentina; or it can move because of changes in productivity. 'Countries with floating exchange rates have seen the largest movements in competitiveness. The UK figures prominently among them. Among the 30 countries that the OECD provides relative unit costs data for, only the USA (during the 1980s) and Mexico (throughout the 80s and 90s) have seen swings in the real exchange rate comparable to those experienced by the UK' (ibid.: 35).

The expression 'loss of competitiveness' is really quite misleading. Sometimes it is accurate – for example, when the real exchange rate moves back to equilibrium after an artificial change in the nominal rate. But the expression can give quite the wrong impression when the real exchange rate appreciates owing to a technological shock: one should see this as a gain in competitiveness in the sector that becomes more productive, and as a loss in competitiveness in sleeping sectors.

The conclusion is the by now familiar one that trying to set the 'right' money exchange rate is a pointless game. The more rigid the economy, the longer it takes for mistakes to be corrected (again a familiar thought – flexibility makes monetary gyrations easier to bear). And if one wants a country to forge ahead on waves of technological innovation it is better to free the exchanges and bite the bullet of losses of competitiveness in backward industries. But more of all this later ...

4(a) The single market: price comparisons

The jury is also out on the matter of the transparency of price comparisons. On the one hand, as Minford points out, the advantage to the consumer of enhanced competition because prices are easier to compare may not be so large for an island whose only land border is with the rural areas of Ireland. Land-border people in the heart of Europe may exercise more market power when they do not have to use a calculator to see who is overcharging them in what currency. On the other hand, there is evidence that price competition is keener in the US than in the larger European countries (HM Treasury, 2003: 60–3). Comparable goods are on the whole cheaper in the USA.

In a labour market made imperfect by unionisation, comparing low wages easily with more productive economies may in the end price out the less productive workers, as is already happening in the former East Germany. Thus there may be few gains in terms of improved price comparisons in goods markets from the UK entering the eurozone, but there may be losses as a result of increased inefficiencies in unionised labour markets.

4(b) The single market: finance

Where the euro is having some effect is in increasing the depth and liquidity of financial markets. Governments and high-credit-rated corporations are finding it easier to place bonds denominated in euros and secondary markets are providing secondary liquidity and narrower spreads. Issuers of paper are also reshaping their strategy to provide larger initial amounts concentrated in a few benchmark maturities. In fact, electronic markets are making commodities out of bonds and trading them increasingly across national borders. Untrammelled competition is working wonders again.

It is typical of the slow way in which the EU works that top-down efforts to unify securities markets are finding almost impassable obstacles. There is a degree of horizontal integration through takeovers of smaller stock exchanges by the Paris and Frankfurt bourses. There is also vertical integration in settlements and security deposit. But, as the reception of the Lamfalussy Report shows, regulatory difficulties are being thrown up by national authorities in ill-conceived attempts to protect national interests (see Lamfalussy et al., 2001).

What is happening is that more governments and corporations, including the British, are issuing paper denominated in euros alongside other denominations. This is as it should be. There will be competition among currencies, not only as a means of payment but also as standards and deposits of value. If in the end financial markets mainly use dollars, yen and euros, so be it.

The location of the wholesale financial services industry, however, is not showing much change: London is and conceivably will be the financial centre of Europe. The currency of the country is not material: all currencies will be used in the City. London has a cluster of financial services industry firms. Language, an able and expert workforce, flexible labour markets, common law and statute law adapted to business needs, a speedy and reliable court system, self-regulation backed by nimble public overseers – these are the strengths of London. It will not be the permanence of sterling as the UK currency which will endanger this predominance. The danger may come from an (unlikely) predominance of centrifugal forces, such as those mentioned by the Treasury Study: technology allowing relocation of routine services offshore, physical infrastructure under stress, high living costs, recruitment problems in boom times.[1] On the whole, London's position as one of the three world financial centres is still unchallenged, with or without the euro.

5 Exchange risk in monetary unions: the alleged volatility of sterling

To think that fixing the exchange rate with the euro will reduce the volatility of the real exchange rate faced by British business is highly contentious. To think that flexible exchange rates impede the growth of trade does not seem to fit the facts.

First let us see what the evidence is on sterling volatility. Minford (2002b: 176–8) starts by assuming that exchange risk has an important effect on real variables, such as trade, foreign direct investment (FDI) or the cost of capital. Since around half of

---

1   HM Treasury, *EMU Study: The Location of Financial Activity and the Euro*, 2000, pp. 1, 2.

Figure 3   **Relative volatility of sterling**
            1990=100

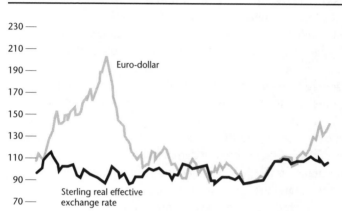

Source: Minford (2002b: 177)

British visible and invisible trade is with the dollar area, it is to be expected that the volatility of the real effective exchange rate of the pound will be lower than that of the euro-dollar rate. This turns out to be the case since 1980, if we substitute the DM for the euro before 1999 (see Figure 3).

If Britain abandons the pound for either the dollar or the euro, then its volatility against the third currency will increase. 'If we remain outside, the pound can ... "go between" the two, rather like someone sitting on the middle of a seesaw.' Indeed, Minford reports that the Liverpool model of the UK economy, when it simulates the difference between floating and under EMU, produces a slightly larger variability in the second case.

Box 5 **The Ricardo-Balassa-Samuelson Effect:
productivity and real exchange rates**

British industrialists often complain that unwanted and
unexpected revaluations possible under flexible exchange
rates can price them out of foreign markets and they
therefore come out in favour of a fixed exchange rate regime.
In other words, many industrialists are in favour of Britain
giving up the pound for the euro and stabilising the relative
value of the euro and the dollar. The belief that exchange rate
fluctuations disappear or are dampened when the money rate
of exchange is fixed or managed is an old mistake. The real
exchange rate does not obey the 'money men', except in so
far as the productivity of the economy may be reduced by
unexpected bouts of inflation caused by political devaluations
of the currency.

David Ricardo, in the second part of Chapter VII, 'On
foreign trade', of his *Principles of Political Economy and
Taxation* (1817), introduced money in his famous model of
Portugal and England, trading wine and cloth. When foreign
trade opens up between the two countries, Portugal being
the more productive in both wine and cloth will export both
and accumulate a balance of gold, which is all that England
can pay with. In consequence, prices rise in Portugal until
the point where England can start exporting cloth, in which
it is relatively less backward. At this point Ricardo introduces
what was later called the 'Balassa-Samuelson theorem'. 'The
improvement of a manufacture in any country tends to alter
the distribution of the precious metals amongst the nations of
the world: it tends to increase the quantity of commodities, at
the same time that it raises the general prices in the country

where the improvement takes place' (ibid.: 141). If exchange rates are fixed, as under the gold standard in Ricardo's time, and today in EMU, prices and wages rise after a productivity shock. If exchange rates float, the currency revalues.

Bela Balassa (1964) and Paul Samuelson (1964) reinterpreted this theorem in a partial equilibrium framework, of the same kind as Ricardo's. When observing deviations in the purchasing power parity of currencies among trading nations, they explained it by arguing that technological progress is faster in traded goods. A rise of productivity in traded goods would lead exporters to bid up wages to attract new workers. Producers of non-traded goods would be forced to increase their relative prices to cover their increased labour costs.

Ricardo's formulation is more elegant and is directly applicable to our explanation of 'revaluations' even when the currency is on a fixed exchange rate regime.

Businesspeople tend to complain about the pound exchange rate volatility. But as was noted above, the real exchange rate tends towards equilibrium, whatever happens to the nominal rate. If market exchange rates are fixed, as under a currency board or under an EMU system, then it is asset prices, wages, interest on credit and cost of supplies which must move.

A fixed exchange rate with the euro will move against the dollar for 50 per cent of Britain's exports, but in fact it will also move against European partners too through changes in British prices. If a revaluation would have occurred when floating, because of a productivity-raising shock, of a technological or a business re-engineering kind, then it will also occur under fixing, through an increase in domestic prices. Both reactions have the same effect of making industries that have not enjoyed the productivity increase more expensive in foreign markets. This currency revaluation mechanism as a response to selective productivity shifts is an incentive for firms to enter the favoured industry (see Box 5). True, revaluations through 'inflation' are usually slower than through currency appreciation, but this is not an advantage. If internal prices are slow to move, then the economy is slower to take advantage of emerging comparative advantage and grows less rapidly, to the ultimate disadvantage of businesses.

One suspects that complaints about volatility of the pound come from industrialists who believe they would prosper with a devaluation.

6 EMU and prospects for British trade

Let us have a look at the British balance of payments, to see whether the UK should price its goods in euros, as the Netherlands does, it being in the different position of a small partner of Germany with a land frontier. Slightly over one half of Britain's foreign commerce in goods and services is with non-EU countries. The value of the current account surplus with the USA and the deficit with the EU will change according to the vagaries of the dollar/euro rate. It is best if the exchange rate finds its own level and does not prejudice either kind of trade (see Figure 4).

A prima facie case can be presented that flexible exchange rates do not seem to have impeded the extraordinary growth of world trade in the last quarter of a century. World exports, from 1972 (when the Bretton Woods system of fixed exchange rates broke down) to 2001, multiplied 6.43 times corrected for GDP growth

Figure 4   **Trade with the EU and the USA**
Credits less debits, £ billion

Current account with the European Union

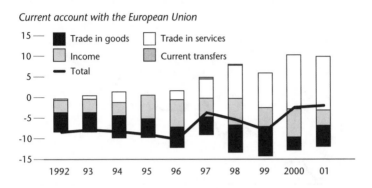

Current account with the USA

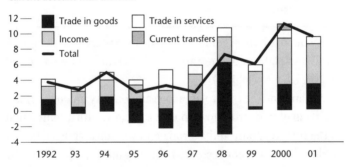

Source: British Department of Trade, *Foreign Trade.*

and 14.58 times in absolute terms. This should be compared with world exports from 1950 to 1971 with fixed exchanges, when they rose 1.79 times corrected for GDP growth and 10 times absolutely.

Andrew K. Rose's paper referred to in Chapter 1 gave weighty reasons, based on the experience of other monetary unions, for

Figure 5   **Irish—British monetary separation and its effect on trade**
Log of volume of trade

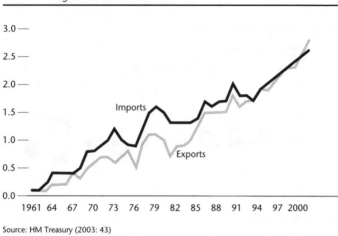

Source: HM Treasury (2003: 43)

believing that EMU would create trade for Britain with the rest of the EU. A notable counter-example is that of trade between Ireland and the UK (see Figure 5).

Ireland and the UK broke a 150-year monetary union in 1979. A sharp fall of trade from 1979 to 1982 coincided with a contraction of the Irish economy and a strong and sustained appreciation of sterling. But trade soon recovered, showing no sign of being hurt by the separation of the punt and the pound. After correcting for the continued fall in the UK's share of Irish trade from the 1960s, in part due to the rapid growth of Ireland and the trade diversion caused by Ireland joining the EU, the authors of the study found that 'the estimated impact of the Anglo-Irish currency regime on trade between the two countries appears insignificantly different from zero' (HM Treasury, 2003: 44). So floating exchange rates may help promote trade – there is certainly no evidence that they hinder trade.

7 Direct investment

Again, there seems to be no decisive evidence that an independent pound is harming the position of the UK as a venue for FDI, although the introduction of the euro is too recent to give any reliable results. The recent figures have also been distorted by the fall in mergers and acquisitions inflow of capital during the 2000/01 American recession. It seems, however, that newspaper headlines echoing the worries of the Japanese that access to the Continental market will be more difficult from Britain if the pound continues to float against the euro should be discounted: see Figure 6.

Given the indecisive nature of the conclusions on this point drawn by the compilers of the Treasury Study, it is best to quote them at some length:

> There is evidence that the UK share of FDI from outside the EU has fallen relative to other EU members since the introduction of the euro. This must however be considered against a backdrop of factors such as the rapid global increase in FDI over the late 1990s, largely driven by M&A activity, and the sharp fall since 2000, as well as the UK leading position within Europe in terms of inward investment. It is difficult to detect with any confidence a specific EMU effect. (ibid.: 67)

8 The dangers of cyclical convergence

After the discussion of optimal currency areas in Chapter 4, the obsession with bringing the British economy in line with the Continent is difficult to share: why would it be a good thing to have the British cycle converge with that of the euro zone?

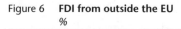

Figure 6   **FDI from outside the EU**
            %

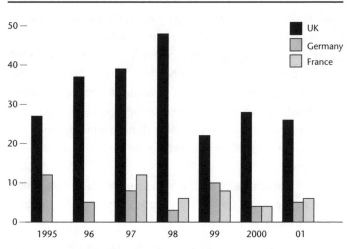

Note: French data not available pre-1997.
Source: HM Treasury (2003: 59).

A cycle is a troublesome phenomenon because variables in an economy that should compensate or counteract each other move in sinister harmony instead: in a slump, prices, wages and interest rates fall; but so do consumption, output, employment and investment, instead of going the other way, as one would expect.

The risk of a worldwide slump would be reduced if there were always countries that bucked the trend. Why should economists seek the convergence that is often regarded as a requirement for or a consequence of joining the eurozone as an end in itself?

9 Seignorage and reserve currency: a step towards politics

Seignorage is not an important tax today. If the point is to have a world currency as one's national money, then this is a question of political pride rather than economic convenience. In that case it would be arguable whether Britain should not establish an orthodox currency board with the dollar or even make the dollar the national currency.

Institutional issues

A number of points midway between economics and politics must be examined before coming to a conclusion. They are framework conditions that would help EMU function more smoothly.

1 Is a Growth and Stability Pact necessary?

The GSP was imposed on those countries accepting full EMU by the Germans, who were afraid that the euro would not be as safe a currency as the DM they had given up. The idea was that governments would keep the amount of public debt below a figure equivalent to 60 per cent of GDP and the budget deficit below 3 per cent of GDP, unless the country were suffering a severe recession. The wording of the pact, however, made the budget figure rather than the proportion of debt the paramount concern.[2]

Now it is the German government, with the backing of the French, that has obtained a temporary suspension of this rule. The president of the Commission, Romano Prodi, has been reported as saying that the GSP was a 'silly rule'. Austria, the

---

2   The pact has been criticised for not taking into consideration the debt load of a country in the application of procedures for breaking the 3 per cent figure. The British argue, for example, that more scope for temporary excessive deficits should be given to countries with lower debt loads.

Netherlands and Finland argued for a firm stance, joined by Sweden and Denmark, which also had a say, albeit no vote on the matter. The most incensed were Spain, Ireland and Portugal, which have made decisive efforts to cut public spending, feeling that tax increases, the other way of balancing the budget, can be counter-productive to long-term growth. The British use a more flexible long-term fiscal framework, allowing deficits to be observed over the whole economic cycle and leaving room for investment finance at all times.

It does seem that the rules of the pact are too rigid and the sanctions perhaps counter-productive: something along the British lines would seem more reasonable, if there were clear ways of forecasting the period and amplitude of cycles. Since such forecasts are subject to political manipulation, it might be better to vary around a positive surplus rather than around zero. Reduced tax intakes during downturns could be accommodated by drawing down net surpluses accumulated in boom times. As Buchanan puts it, 'pre-Keynesian fiscal principles ... supported a budget surplus during normal times to provide a cushion for more troublesome periods' (Buchanan and Wagner, 1977: 11). There are two reasons for this kind of solution. One is that a continual reduction of debt provides pressure to cut back public expenditure, equivalent today to 40 or 50 per cent or more in advanced economies: levels that are a clear and unnecessary inroad into personal freedoms and entrepreneurial initiative. The other is that 'effective democratic government requires institutional arrangements that force citizens to take account of the costs of government as well as the benefits, and to do so simultaneously' (ibid.: 12).

Also, it is clear that the EU will not let any member state go

Box 6 The Growth and Stability Pact

The object and procedures of the Growth and Stability Pact were agreed at the European Council of 1997 in Amsterdam. In compliance with the Pact:

(a) the member states:

- would undertake to comply with the medium-term budgetary objective of positions close to balance or in surplus;
- were invited to make public, on their own initiative, the Council recommendations made to them;
- committed themselves to taking the corrective budgetary action they deemed necessary to meet the objectives of their stability or convergence programmes;
- without delay, on receiving information indicating the risk of a deficit exceeding 3% of GDP, would launch the corrective budgetary adjustments they deemed necessary;
- would correct excessive deficits as quickly as possible after their emergence;
- undertook not to invoke the exceptional nature of a deficit linked to an annual fall in GDP of less than 2% unless they were in severe recession (annual fall in real GDP of at least 0.75%).

(b) the Commission:

- would first issue a 'preventive warning' to the non-complying member states;
- then a 'warning of excessive deficit';
- and finally would address an opinion and a recommendation to the Council concerning the lack of compliance by the member states.

(c) the Council:
- if within four months effective action is not taken or the excessive deficit is not corrected within one year, the Council gives notice to the member state concerned.
- No later than two months after notice has been given, the Council normally decides to impose sanctions if the member state fails to comply with the Council's decisions.
- Sanctions first take the form of a non-interest-bearing deposit with the Commission. The amount of this deposit comprises:
  - a fixed component equal to 0.2% of GDP;
  - a variable component equal to one tenth of the difference between the deficit as a percentage of GDP in the year in which the deficit was deemed to be excessive and the reference value of 3% of GDP. A deposit is as a rule converted into a fine if, in the view of the Council, the excessive deficit has not been corrected after two years.

Up to now four member states have been warned by the Commission. Two have complied: Ireland, despite a large budget surplus, for expansive policies when suffering inflation; Portugal for a large and previously hidden budget deficit. Two notoriously have not: Germany budgeted a deficit of 3.2% of GDP for 2002, 3.1% for 2003, and foresees more than 3% for 2004; France hovered around 3% for the years 2002 and 2003, and has forecast 3.5% for 2004. In spite of that, and in spite of these countries not presenting plans for correction, the European Council decided on 25 November 2003 not to apply sanctions.

bankrupt. The market therefore is sure that rogue states will be baled out, and so are the rogue states themselves. This moral hazard would increase the risk margin on a member state's public debt and if pushed too far could lead to an Argentinian sort of disaster.

If the objective is stable money one must not simply rely on rules and regulations imposed by civil servants and politicians on a monopoly central bank. Competition is needed to ensure that persistent transgressors pursuing poor policy will suffer a reduction in the demand for their currency and a fall in their seignorage earnings. Other things being equal, one of the strongest arguments for keeping sterling is that it makes the ECB face institutional competition, both in Europe and worldwide.

2 Labour market reform

The euro zone labour market is not well adapted to the needs of a progressive economy. The most visible example is the French 35-hour week. But, in general, labour market flexibility is lacking on the Continent (see Figure 7).

A freer labour market does not prevent transversal or asymmetric shocks but allows markets to produce their innovative effects without the cost of a sizeable increase in unemployment. Hence the 'natural rate' of unemployment is higher in the euro zone than in more flexible countries. This structural unemployment is compatible with different inflation rates, cannot be reduced by an inflationary policy, and will respond to changes in labour laws.

Deep labour market reform is not likely in the euro zone.

Figure 7   **The EU labour market compared**
Indicator score

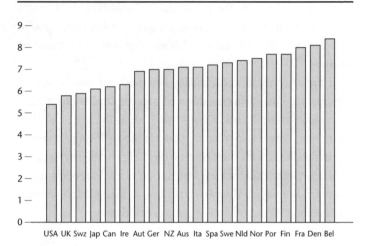

USA UK Swz Jap Can Ire Aut Ger NZ Aus Ita Spa Swe Nld Nor Por Fin Fra Den Bel

Note: A lower value implies a more flexible institutional environment.
Source: HM Treasury, 2003

3 The impending pension crisis

The Maastricht rules hide the real extent of member states'
indebtedness. Only the Netherlands and the UK have manageable pension liabilities. According to a paper circulated by the
European Commission, many European governments would show
debts of more than 100 per cent of GDP on their balance sheets if
these were honestly compiled.[3]

---

3   A study of 27 November 2003 quoted by *The Economist* calculates staggering total
    public debt for most advanced countries. A. K. Frederiksen in Heller (2003) cal-
    culates implicit debt from pension, health and environmental liabilities equiva-
    lent to almost 400 per cent of GDP for Canada, nearly 300 per cent for Spain,
    down to 150 per cent for France and Germany; while Britain's total debt, explicit
    and hidden, is just over 100 per cent of GDP. The exact figures may be hard to
    calculate, but the liabilities are there.

State pension yearly shortfall came to around 10 per cent of GDP in the three largest EU states. Spain is showing a cash surplus due in the most part to immigrants entering the legal labour force. The bulk of these immigrant low earners, however, are expected to draw total benefits over the years larger than their contributions.

Now, there are only five measures that can be taken to lighten a problem that promises to get worse with the ageing of the population. The first four of these are: to reduce pension rights; to increase social insurance contributions and taxes; to increase the retiring age; and to recognise the debt, issue bonds to finance it and privatise pensions without reneging on promises. The fourth is the least likely and all the others will be adopted half-heartedly. The fifth measure is for the countries with problems to create inflation ...

Economic arguments and the *six* tests

The British government is on record as being clearly in favour of membership of the single currency, but economic conditions must be right before joining. These conditions have been summarised in the five tests as set out by the Chancellor of the Exchequer.

This is a quick review of the five conditions before the extra condition relating to trade was added.

• Test 1: Sustainable *convergence* between Britain and the economies of a single currency. The two cycles are still out of sync and, according to the Treasury, full harmony between the British and Continental growth patterns is not around the corner. Much will depend on the judgement of the civil servants and the Chancellor of the Exchequer, but the macroeconomies of other countries in the euro zone, such as Spain and Ireland, are also at odds with those of the core countries, and the system seems to take these disharmonies in its stride.

- Test 2: Whether there is sufficient *flexibility* to cope with economic change. The trouble will come for the rigid Continental economies, not for the UK economy. Britain will be able to ride the wave, if some further reforms are carried out.

- Test 3: The effect on *investment* – fully joining the euro zone could make the UK an attractive venue for foreign investors wanting to enjoy the advantages of being in Britain and in the euro at the same time – along the lines of FDI in Ireland.

- Test 4: The impact on the *financial services* industry. The City must not suffer from the switch to the euro, but it is believed the City will gain clients by using the currency of the huge EU market, to be increased by new accessions. Implicit is the assertion that the City will remain a European and world-class financial centre only if its main unit of account is the euro; and that London being part of the euro zone will help make the euro a real world currency.

- Test 5: Whether the euro is good for *employment*. The great worry in joining a monetary zone that is not optimal is that transversal shocks, as they are called, will create high unemployment in rigid economies. But Britain's labour market is the most flexible in the EU, so the worry is exaggerated, and in any case the remedy is within the hands of the British, who can repeal some legal restrictions on employment.

On 9 June 2003, the Chancellor reviewed the state of fulfilment of the five criteria in a statement in Parliament. One was found to have been reached: 'So we conclude the financial services test is met. We still have to meet the two tests of sustainable convergence and flexibility. Subject to the achievement of sustainable convergence and sufficient flexibility, the tests for investment and employment would be met.'[4]

A noticeable addition to the five tests is the effect of the euro on trade, which conceivably could be unfavourable. The contentious conclusion of the Treasury Study is that the effect of full EMU would be unequivocally positive.

> The assessment shows that intra-euro area trade has increased strongly in recent years as a result of EMU, perhaps by as much as 3 to 20 per cent; that the UK could enjoy a significant boost to trade with the euro area of up to 50 per cent over 30 years; and that UK national income could rise over a 30-year period by between 5 and 9 per cent. A 9 per cent increase in national income would translate into a boost to potential output of around $\frac{1}{4}$ percentage point a year, sustained over a 30-year period. (HM Treasury, 2003)

The Chancellor promised that a new assessment of the tests would be carried out in 2004 and a draft Referendum Bill published in the autumn of 2004.

He also promised to carry out some structural reforms to make the passing of the tests easier and quicker: a new inflation target; reform of the housing market, in matters of planning, supply and long-term mortgages; changes in fiscal reporting to Parliament

---

4   Statement of the Chancellor of the Exchequer on UK Membership of the Single Currency, House of Commons, 9 June 2003.

and in assessing the local impact of public pay agreements; further flexibility in labour, product and capital markets; review of the exchange rate and the fiscal and monetary mix; and reconsideration of the Stability and Growth Pact and reform of the European Central Bank – quite a programme!

Chancellor Brown has presented his five (in fact six) tests as if there were total certainty that they will be fulfilled some day soon; and as if, once fulfilled, there would then be no further questions, economic or political, to be asked. Brown's criteria are *suspensive* in that they simply put off the day of decision until economic convergence and flexibility have increased enough to make the costs of transition to the euro negligible.

By formulating and stressing these suspensive conditions as the only ones to be worth mentioning, the Chancellor is making two implicit assumptions which we consider explicitly below. They are:

1 That in good time the transitional economic disadvantages of full EMU for Britain will have been addressed satisfactorily.
2 That the long-run advantages to giving up sterling and adopting the euro are beyond dispute.

If one looks at the Chancellor's tests closely, as we have done in these pages, the likelihood of their being fulfilled appears remote.

• Tests 1 and 2: Convergence and flexibility. As Patrick Minford puts it, these two tests amount to finding out whether the UK will go back to an alternation between 'booms and busts' by adopting the euro. There is no useful way of trying this out in practice, since adopting the euro is irreversible. By using the

Box 7 **State of the five tests in June 2003 according to the Chancellor**

Convergence

Are business cycles and economic structures compatible so that we and others could live comfortably with euro interest rates on a permanent basis?

There has been significant progress on convergence since 1997, which marks a break with the UK's past history of divergence and reflects greater stability of the UK economy and global trends towards integration. Indeed, the UK now exhibits a greater degree of cyclical convergence than some EMU members demonstrated in the run-up to the start of EMU in 1999 and remains more convergent than a number of EMU countries today. The UK meets the EC Treaty convergence criteria for inflation, long-term interest rates and government deficits and debt. But there remain structural differences with the euro area, some of which are significant, such as in the housing market. Because of the risks these factors pose, and the fact that any dynamic changes would take time to come through, we cannot yet be confident that UK business cycles are sufficiently compatible with those of the euro area to allow the UK to live comfortably with euro area interest rates on a permanent basis. Overall, at the present time, while the extent of convergence with the euro area has significantly increased, the convergence test is not met. The Government is committed to building on the platform of stability and has announced a wide-ranging forward-looking policy agenda to deliver high levels of output and employment. This will help to make the economy more convergent with the euro area for the future.

Flexibility

If problems emerge is there sufficient flexibility to deal with them?

UK labour market flexibility has improved markedly since 1997. Significant falls in unemployment have accompanied strong employment growth giving the UK one of the lowest levels of unemployment in the OECD, lower even than in the US. While considerable progress has been made to reform labour, product and capital markets in the UK and the euro area, more can be done to ensure the UK economy is resilient to deal with the risks identified in the convergence test and the challenges of EMU membership. Inflation volatility is very likely to increase inside EMU. Greater flexibility in the UK and throughout the euro area would minimise output and employment instability, helping to ensure convergence was durable and that the potential benefits of EMU could be fully realised. This underlines the importance of maintaining progress on a range of economic reform policies to enhance flexibility and resilience to shocks, particularly in labour markets. The less progress on flexibility that is achieved in the EU, the greater the premium on a high level of flexibility in the UK economy. Overall, at the present time, we cannot be confident that UK flexibility, while improved, is sufficient. Reflecting this, at the present time, the achievement of sustainable and durable convergence has not been demonstrated. But increased flexibility through the measures we set out will help to provide greater reassurance that the economy can meet the additional demands that EMU membership would pose and contribute to achieving sustainable and durable convergence.

Investment

Would joining EMU create better conditions for firms making long-term decisions to invest in Britain?

UK productivity has been held back by a legacy of long-term under-investment. EMU entry could reduce the cost of capital for UK firms if long-term interest rates fell further inside the euro area and if membership of a larger financial market reduced the cost of finance. These costs could fall for small and medium-sized enterprises (SMEs) – in particular if joining EMU lowers the barriers which prevent SMEs accessing euro area financial markets and lowers the cost of bank lending. Over time, EMU is likely to boost cross-border investment flows and foreign direct investment (FDI) in the euro area. There has been a fall in the UK's share of total EU FDI flows coinciding with the start of EMU, and a corresponding increase in the share of the euro area. But against the backdrop of many other influences on FDI flows, it is difficult to say with confidence that EMU has boosted FDI within the euro area. There can, however, be confidence that a successfully operating EMU, and UK membership of it on the right basis, would boost FDI over the longer term. There is a risk that the longer membership of the euro is delayed, the longer the potential gains in terms of increased inward investment are postponed. If sustainable and durable convergence is achieved, then we can be confident that the quantity and quality of investment would increase, ensuring that the investment test was met.

Financial services

What impact would entry into EMU have on the competitive position of the UK's financial services industry, particularly the City's wholesale markets?

Over the four years since the start of EMU, the UK has attracted a significant level of wholesale financial services business. The strength of the City in international wholesale financial services activity should mean that it continues to do so, whether inside or outside EMU. EMU entry should enhance the already strong competitive position of the UK's wholesale financial services sector by offering some additional benefits. Again, while the UK's retail financial services sector should remain competitive either inside or outside the euro area, entry would offer greater potential to compete and capture the effects of greater EU integration that would arise from the single currency and other efforts to complete the Single Market, in particular the Financial Services Action Plan (FSAP) – benefits which are postponed while the UK is not in EMU. Overall, the financial services test is met.

Growth, stability and employment

In summary, will joining EMU promote higher growth, stability and a lasting increase in jobs?

EMU membership could significantly raise UK output and lead to a lasting increase in jobs in the long term. As noted above, the assessment shows that intra-euro area trade has increased strongly in recent years as a result of EMU, perhaps by as much as 3 to 20 per cent; that the UK could enjoy a significant boost to trade with the euro area of up to 50 per cent over 30 years; and that UK national income could rise over a 30-year period by between 5 and 9 per cent. A 9 per cent increase in national income would translate into a boost to potential output of around $\frac{1}{4}$ percentage point a year, sustained over a 30-year period. Despite the progress made since 1997, the lack of sustainable and durable convergence means that, for the UK, macroeconomic stability would be harder to maintain inside EMU than outside, were the UK to make a decision to join at the present time. The potential uncertainty created by the price stability objective of the European Central Bank (ECB) and the potential constraints on the use of fiscal policy for stabilisation under the current interpretation of the Stability and Growth Pact (SGP) increase the chances that output and employment would be less stable inside EMU. The Government supports the direction in which the EU macroeconomic framework is evolving. Enhancing the flexibility and dynamism of the European economy, building on the achievements of the economic reform programme agreed at Lisbon, will also be important if the full benefits of EMU are to be realised. Entering EMU on the basis of sustainable and durable convergence is essential so that the UK can benefit from the substantial increases in cross-border trade, investment, competition and productivity that EMU could provide. Lower prices would lead to a lower cost of living, a key potential benefit of EMU entry for households, but one that would only accrue if entry were on the basis of sustainable and durable convergence. Poorer households tend to spend a greater proportion of their income on goods and services, so lower prices could benefit such households relatively more than wealthier ones. Overall, we can be confident that the growth, stability and employment test would be met once sustainable and durable convergence has been achieved.

Overall the Treasury assessment is that since 1997 the UK has made real progress towards meeting the five economic tests. But, on balance, though the potential benefits of increased investment, trade, a boost to financial services, growth and jobs are clear, we cannot at this point in time conclude that there is sustainable and durable convergence or sufficient flexibility to cope with any potential difficulties within the euro area. So, despite the risks and costs from delaying the benefits of joining, a clear and unambiguous case for UK membership of EMU has not at the present time been made and a decision to join now would not be in the national economic interest.

Source: Statement by the Chancellor of the Exchequer on UK Membership of the Single Currency, 9 June 2003, House of Commons.

'Liverpool model of the British Economy' and bombarding it at random with the kinds of shock typical of recent British history, Professor Minford expects the present variability factor induced to increase by 75 per cent under full EMU conditions (Minford, 2002b: 180).

- Test 3: Investment. The currency seems to have no effect whatsoever on FDI and there is no reason why national investment should be affected.
- Test 4: Financial services. London is still the capital of the European financial system, dealing in all currencies as the need arises and profit dictates. Brussels rules and

regulations may reduce its attractiveness compared with New York.

- Test 5: Employment. Here it is not the euro itself, but EMU, Economic and Monetary Union, of which the euro is a part, and which includes the imposition of labour market rules, which will directly lead to more unemployment.
- And Test 6: Trade. The jury is still out on whether the euro will lead to an increase in trade between the UK and the rest of Europe without affecting trade with the rest of the world. The Irish case seems to show that commerce is little influenced by the currency in which goods and services are traded.

However, even if the Chancellor's suspensive conditions were fulfilled and there was no need any more to put the euro on hold, we would still want to be sure that adopting the euro would be for the good of Britain; we would want to be sure that the balance of benefit would be *sufficient* to take the jump. This has not been proven. It is quite possible that the Chancellor of the Exchequer's tests will be passed, but our economic analysis suggests that they are the wrong 'tests'.

7 SUMMARY OF THE ECONOMIC ARGUMENTS FOR AND AGAINST KEEPING STERLING

Here we sum up the economic arguments for and against Britain giving up the pound for the euro and conclude where the greater benefit lies.

Let us take the topics listed in Table 3 one by one.

1 The question of whether the euro zone, with or without Britain and Scandinavia, will ever be an optimal currency area is not well posed. Continental friends of the euro hope that European economies will soon converge so that a single monetary policy is feasible in the euro zone. British opponents of the euro have underlined the difficulty of a centralised monetary policy in a currency area that is not optimal. We have argued that the whole concept of an optimal currency area is not important.

Optimality of currency management, in the sense of the central bank policy having the same proportional effect over all individuals and firms, is an oxymoron. Aiming for it can easily become a hindrance rather than a help, because of moral hazard, when the general public get accustomed to counting on monetary policy to mend their personal mistakes. Monetary policy must aim at creating a steady standard so that the currency is suitably stable and liquid. Attempts to manage the real economic cycle (or to put in place a '*Konjunkturpolitik*', as the Germans say) are in any case futile. Nimble adaptation to changing economic conditions is more desirable than sluggish change in a harmonised optimal currency area.

2 The long-term value of the currency is what matters. It could be better protected under the British dispensation, which originated in the Maastricht Treaty: the Bank of England enjoys a balance between central bank independence and democratic account-ability that the ECB lacks. If the management of the pound sterling were to prove deficient, the economy would become 'euro-ised', just as some Latin American economies have become dollarised, which in a way is what the adoption of the euro has meant for some Continental economies.

3 The euro leads towards economic convergence, institutional integration and social harmonisation, which is precisely what the EU does not need. The existence of the pound contributes to monetary and institutional competition, and is thus a force for social variety.

4 The prosperity of the City of London does not seem to have been affected by Britain keeping the pound. If financial costs can be reduced by dealing in a single currency, then the market will induce governments, corporations, funds and final investors to issue and accept euro-denominated paper. The key to which currency, if not both, will be principally used is liquidity and the cost of transacting.

5 There is indeed a cost saving in using the same set of notes and coins as the rest of the euro zone, but this saving loses importance

Table 3 **Summary of the economic arguments for adopting the euro or keeping the pound**

Adopting the € throughout the EU

1   As EMU helps economies converge, Britain will soon find itself part of an optimal currency area

2   German-style monetary policy carried out by a self-regulating ECB answerable to nobody

3   The € is a force for economic convergence, institutional integration and social harmonisation

4   Financial standardisation imposed by Frankfurt and Brussels will reduce financial transactions costs

5   Transactions costs of using physical currency will be reduced by adopting the euro

6   Seignorage from a € used worldwide will be shared among member states according to their GDP. € denominated government bonds enjoy greater liquidity

7   Easier price comparison makes for keener competition

8   No £/€ exchange risk frees business from windfall losses

9   If the exchange rate at entry is well chosen, there will be no induced initial boom or recession

10 Comparative studies of EU countries seem to reveal that EMU will lead directly to increased trade with the euro zone

11 The adoption of the € would make Britain a bridgehead for outside investors in the euro zone

12 The Growth and Stability Pact will induce a reform of Continental welfare systems

13 By adopting the € Britain will contribute to a politically stronger and economically better-controlled Union

Keeping the £, the kronas and the Swiss franc	Balance
Currency area optimality, if attainable, is not advisable; better heed the lessons of asymmetric shocks than alleviate their effects by spreading them across the EU	£
Bank of England autonomous Monetary Policy Committee, with ultimate reference to the Chancellor of the Exchequer	£
The £ contributes to institutional and monetary competition, and social variety. Harmonising and centralising will give rise to new interventionism	£
Competition among financial centres has reinforced the City of London's prosperity	£
The spread of electronic money will also reduce transactions costs without the one-off costs of monetary unification	=
Small reliable currencies such as the Swiss franc can obtain large seignorage benefits. Spread reduction will only be considerable for previously profligate nations	€
Price comparison would be effective chiefly in border areas; but the wage demonstration effect could equalise labour costs upwards	€
Adopting € would induce greater trade-weighted £ volatility, especially affecting the 50 per cent of British trade carried on in $.	£
Despite an alleged proneness to overshooting, floating is less disruptive than the likelihood of fixing the wrong rate	=
More reliable individual country studies (e.g. Ireland before and after monetary union with Britain) show no effect of monetary union on trade	=
Statistics show no evidence of FDI being affected by monetary diversity	=
Pension liabilities in the euro zone counsel keeping well away from a currency undermined by huge hidden debts	£
A € playing the role of gold from 1870 until World War I and embedded in a free-market Europe would lessen worries about losing monetary control	£

with the spread of electronic money; and the present value of the saving on transactions is offset by the present value of the change-over cost.

6 If the euro becomes a world currency, seignorage can be large. There is quasi-seignorage to be gained as euro-denominated government bonds of small and previously untrustworthy member states come to be traded in more liquid markets and with narrower spreads. Even small currencies can earn a considerable amount of seignorage, however – witness the Swiss franc.

7 There is no need for all consumers to be aware of price differences for euro-price competition to have an effect: price convergence is driven by marginal suppliers or consumers trading outside their borders because of the possibility of arbitrage gains. Prices of non-tradable goods would be higher in more productive economies (see Box 5). Trade unions would use wage comparisons as arguments for wage hikes. On balance, however, a single currency would foster competition.

8 There is no such thing as 'no exchange risk'. Even if the money exchange rate is fixed, real costs will respond to international conditions. 'Tradables' will be valued at world prices. The prices of 'non-tradables' will in the end respond to money created by balance of payments deficits or surpluses, especially so when there is no national central bank, as is the case in the euro zone. A currency in the middle of the euro and the dollar would be less volatile.

9 Only if, by chance, the right rate is chosen will adopting the

euro not endanger steady growth. If the 'wrong' rate is chosen, the effects will be different if the country is able to reform the economy so as to make it flexible. A 'favourable' entry rate (whereby the local currency is effectively devalued against the euro) can be followed by real growth, as was the case for Spain, or by inflation and stagnation, as happened in Portugal, depending on whether the necessary economic reforms are carried out. Floating is the more prudent choice for Britain.

10 The trade between Ireland and Britain is an *experimentum crucis* for the alleged influence of monetary union on trade: giving up a secular currency union has had no perceptible effect on the growth of commerce.

11 Again, there is no statistical evidence for the belief that currency denomination has any effect on foreign investment, be it direct or financial.

12 The Growth and Stability Pact is being questioned by France, Germany and Italy precisely to postpone the day of reckoning on dysfunctional welfare systems and labour market regulation. And the euro zone's zero deficit rule, since it is applied to current budgets, does not include the hidden debt of pay-as-you-go pensions and an ageing population's medical demands – a euro-debt that may tempt the ECB to reduce the value of the currency in ten or twenty years' time.

13 The thesis of this essay is that, if joining the euro meant entering a truly free-market area, then many of the above objections might lose weight and giving up sterling might be worth the risk. But the

euro zone is more like a *Zollverein* along the lines of the Prussian empire than part of a *laissez-faire, laissez-passer* gold standard world.

In sum, the only economic arguments relatively *in favour of the euro for Britain* are: the greater ease with which British workers, consumers and firms can compare wages and prices with those in other parts of Europe; seignorage income if euro notes and coins are used by non-Europeans; and quasi-seignorage gains by governments if euro-bonds are more keenly demanded by savers in the EU and the world at large.

On a number of counts, the points are evenly shared: transactions cost gains are reduced by the cost of changeover and by the spread of electronic money; and there seems to be no economic advantage to be gained on the counts of the entry rate of exchange, or the effect on trade and investment.

The balance of the economic argument appears to be *in favour of keeping sterling*: striving for euro area optimality works against productivity; the monetary policy rule of the Bank of England is as good as or better than that of the ECB; the pound promotes institutional competition; the City of London seems to be prospering under a monetary competition regime; exchange rate risk would increase for the UK with the euro; and a different currency will preserve Britain from the fall-out of a public pension and health service crisis on the Continent. The UK government does not reflect these important economic issues in its tests, however.

The euro may be more acceptable on the Continent, where so many currencies were of bad quality, as evidenced by the interest rate spread against the DM. But one must reach a different conclusion if the question is whether to give up the pound. The only factor that could overrule this economic conclusion would be if the political advantages were so great as to make the cost of changing worthwhile. Hence, the political side of the question becomes paramount. To this we must now turn.

Part 4
The *Political* Case for Keeping Sterling

The man of system seems to imagine that he can arrange the different members of a great society with as much ease as the hand arranges the different pieces upon a chess-board ... But, in the great chessboard of human society, every single piece has a principle of motion of its own.

ADAM SMITH, *THE THEORY OF MORAL SENTIMENTS*, 1759

Matters of currency have always been politically charged. A stable money is of great importance to merchants, consumers, savers, employers and workers, but authorities, under the guise of managing money for the good of the people, have always tried to enlist this powerful instrument to their own ends. Now it is the turn of the euro, which, under the pretext of giving Europeans a safe means of payment, is impressed in the cause of making the EU more efficient and compact.

The economics of giving up sterling for the euro boil down to how reliable and acceptable a system is being built in the euro zone. The Growth and Stability Pact is under a cloud. The welfare systems on the Continent, with the possible exception of that in the Netherlands, will end in disaster, unless fundamentally amended. The Brussels-controlled economy is worlds away from the full competition, free trade and balanced budgets of the golden era of the gold standard.

If the euro were a means to supply Europeans with a stable currency, helping to foster personal and business autonomy, along the lines of a pre-World War I gold standard, then Britain could contemplate adopting it for the sake of long-run prosperity and social progress (Minford, 2002a: 64). But, politically speaking, if sterling and monetary and institutional competition are to be surrendered to further the kind of centralising Europe outlined in the Versailles Convention chaired by M. Giscard d'Estaing, then the answer must be No. The pound can still do sterling work for individual freedom in Europe.

8 MONOPOLY MONEY AND POLITICAL CENTRALISATION

We must now answer two political questions: what is the connection between European Monetary Union and European political union? And what are the dangers of a single currency for the EU?

Can monetary union exist without a central political power?

Experts differ as to whether a monetary union must be backed by a strong central state or a political union, because they have tended to confuse the creation of a monetary union where a single currency is legal tender with the spontaneous circulation of an international currency worldwide. The verdict of history is clear but has not been properly read by historians. It is not widely understood that the role of the issuer of a new currency imposed by political agreement within a monetary union is fundamentally different from that of the guarantor of a currency that people inside and outside the area will demand if it suits them. In the first case, experience shows that some sort of political union is necessary if the monetary union and the single currency are to last. In the second case, a world currency will be accepted outside the area where the political writ of the issuer runs, if there is some guarantee that its quality will last. In this second case you still need a state for a fiat currency to survive, but the crucial point is how to transform one of these state currencies into an international currency, voluntarily used by traders around the world. Abolishing legal tender within the borders of the state whose currency aspires to be widely used will certainly help.

The wide circulation of money with a face value greater than its commodity value is the source of seignorage for the issuer (see Box 1). Even in times of commodity money, the trusted issuer was able to stamp a face value on a silver or gold coin greater than the value of the metal because it relieved traders from weighing and assaying the piece they received in payment. There was the tacit agreement that the coin was of a certain weight and fineness, so that the holder could always resort to melting it to exercise the implicit guarantee.

When private banks started issuing notes promising that they would be ready to exchange them for gold or silver at par and on demand, the reliability of the issuer was an even more important element in the acceptability of this new paper money. Later, governments stepped in, granting banknote monopolies to central banks in exchange for loans; the backing of the state often added a guarantee that the bank would fulfil its liquidity promise. Further down the road central banknotes were decreed inconvertible and legal tender, so that the state moved from guaranteeing the value of the notes to imposing their use within its sovereign territory.

In the period of commodity money it was not necessary that a strong central state should underpin the value of coins widely used in trade: in fact, there could be and there were currencies issued by small merchant republics with relatively little political power, as long as their money had the reputation of being sterling. Thus the florin, named after the republic of Florence, and the ducat, after the duchy of Venice, were international money on the shores of the Mediterranean, for two reasons not directly connected with political power. They were convenient for trading with the merchants of those commercial republics and their gold and silver content was expected not to change.

The general displacement of commodity money by state fiat money with a value unrelated to a commodity has had the effect of forcing states to make the national currency legal standard. If there was the desire to make the national commodity international, so as to reap additional seignorage, then some kind of additional guarantee of its continuing value had to be proffered. Since the temptation to abuse the sovereign power of legal tender is almost irresistible, the self-denying ordinance against over-issue had to be credible, especially in a newly created money. The euro in consequence has had to be launched with a triple condition: that the central bank should keep inflation at a minimum; that the central bank should not become 'the banker of the government'; and that the fledgling political union should have the power to prevent rogue member states from free-riding on the reputation of the currency.

Spontaneous world currencies versus imposed national currencies

It is one thing to have a currency used spontaneously beyond the domains of the issuing authority and quite another to create a monetary union. In the first case, the coin in itself enjoys the reputation that it is a safe currency and has a readily exchangeable value not much smaller than the face value assigned to it by the mint. In the case of a monetary union, different states agree to grant exclusive legal-tender status to the common currency, making it in effect a fiat money.

There are many examples of world currencies spontaneously accepted in trade and for domestic transactions. It is a question of the degree of confidence the currency in question inspires, either because it has commodity value or because it is widely accepted as more stable than other means of payment. The use of the Spanish doubloon or of the Maria Theresa thaler spread well beyond the political borders of the authority coining them; so has the use of the dollar bill, which has become the effective currency in countries such as Panama and Guatemala and effective legal-tender money in countries such as Ecuador and El Salvador.

The kingdom of Castile and the viceroyalties and captaincies of the Indies had a three-tier monetary system: a unit of account that did not circulate, the *maravedí*; the gold and silver coins, variously denominated as *escudos* and *ducados* when made of gold, and *reales* when made of silver; a fiat money made of inflatable copper coins called *moneda de vellón*, or 'bullion' money. An analysis of this three-tiered system is of great help in understanding why the backing of a state is not the crucial element for the international acceptance of a currency. It also shows how the spontaneous use of good-quality money can easily extend beyond the writ of the prince whose profile is stamped on the coins.

The *maravedí*, defined as a fraction of the gold commodity money, went out of use as an actual coin in the first part of the fifteenth century but was kept as a unit of account to standardise the relative value of the pieces variously used in the realm: gold, silver and copper (see García Guerra, 2000: 575–7).

The value and weight of the Castilian gold and silver coins were set by Queen Isabella of Castile and King Ferdinand of Aragon in

1497, an arrangement that lasted, with few important changes, until the end of the seventeenth century. The principal denomination of the gold coins was that of *ducado*, indicating an intention to build on the reputation of the Venetian ducat, and that of the silver coin, the *real*. The doubloon or double ducat became the eponymous gold coin. For silver, it was the *real de a ocho* (or 'piece of eight') which circulated throughout the world, even as far as China, under various names, mainly that of 'Spanish dollar'. Throughout those two centuries, the kings of Spain refrained from tampering with the value of their international currency, except by adapting it to the changing value of silver versus gold, and this despite the fact that the Spanish treasury suspended payments or declared bankruptcy no fewer than nine times from 1557 to 1662.[1] It was not the power of the Spanish crown which maintained the currency of the Castilian *ducados* and *reales*, but the constancy of their metal exchangeable value and the importance of the kingdom of Castile in Europe and in America, as a commercial partner. The might of the Spanish state played a role only in the ability of the mints of Castile and the Indies to keep producing those pieces of precious metal, thanks to the productivity of the Spanish mines.[2] A commodity money has a value independently of the decrees of the issuer.

---

[1] On other counts there were eleven suspensions: 1557, 1575 and 1596, under Philip II; 1607 under Philip III; 1627, 1647, 1652, 1660 and 1662 under Philip IV; and two feint ones in 1667 and 1676/77 under Charles II. Some of these suspensions were not due to lack of silver for the Crown but to the need to negotiate new terms with the Castilian, German, Genoese and Portuguese bankers: see Sanz Ayán (2000).

[2] Castile became a virtual monopolist of silver production thanks to a new refining technique: instead of having to toast the pyrites by heating them with scarce wood, the precious metal in the sulphates was displaced by mercury, of which Castile had abundant supplies in Almadén, south of Madrid, and Huancavélica, in Peru.

In fact the Spanish Crown was far from blameless in matters of money. The power of the state was used to impose the circulation of copper money in Castile. The power of the state, however, could not prevent the constant devaluation of the *vellón* with respect to silver owing to its over-issue. From 1602 until 1685, the Spanish Crown financed a considerable part of its military expenses with an inflation tax on bullion money. There were two attempts at monetary reform, in 1628 and 1642, but continual wars led to more inflationary finance. Throughout the century, theologians and pamphleteers denounced inflationary copper issue and explained the connection of the abuse of *vellón* money by the king with its depreciation, with the silver premium and with price inflation. Copper money was finally devalued and its production discontinued in the more peaceful 1680s, and inflation conquered (see Santiago Fernández, 2000). A fiat money is more easily tampered with than a commodity money.

This story shows that the interference of a powerful but penurious state is the worst thing that can happen to a currency. The kings of Castile did not tamper unduly with the unit of account, the *maravedí*; neither did they greatly change the metal content of the doubloons and pieces of eight, so they became the world commercial currency until displaced by other sources of the precious metals. The Spanish state used its power where it dared, by issuing *vellón* in excess. Why, then, does Robert Mundell suggest that 'a strong central state' will help the euro become an international money? Is the need for the heavy hand of a strong European state not a bad omen for the future of the euro? Is it not true that the possibility that it will be displaced as an international means of payment by the competition of other currencies is the only relative guarantee that the euro will not depreciate too far?

The fate of previous monetary unions

A monetary union of the monopolistic sort is greatly exposed to abuse by free riders. When the monetary union is built on the mere fixing of exchange rates among different currencies enjoying legal tender, crises of the sort that afflicted the European monetary system are probable, even likely. This is because each of the various sovereign issuers of money will be tempted to take advantage of the fact that their money is, by virtue of the fixed exchange rates, legal tender over the whole union.

Even when a single currency holds sway throughout the area, the persistence of national treasuries with independent fiscal powers, and the existence of different credit and bank supervision policies, will give rise to frictions that may lead to the break-up of the union. If one of the states of the monetary union follows an imprudent fiscal or supervisory policy, there is a danger that the reputation of the single currency will be tainted by the unreliability of one member. True, the effect of fiscal policy on the currency is much slower than the effect of competitive over-issue, but unless it is clear that the rogue state will be left to go bankrupt if it behaves profligately, the credibility of the single currency will suffer. A Growth and Stability Pact will almost surely not be enough: the monetary history of the USA shows, in the words of the Dutch economist Wim Vanthoor, that 'fiscal discipline was only brought about by the absence of any obligation of Federal Government to support an individual state in the case of a financial crisis'.[3]

Vanthoor, in his learned book about European monetary unions, distinguishes two kinds: supra-regional and inter-European. The supra-regional unions are Switzerland in 1848, Italy

---

3   Vanthoor (1996: 129), quoting Jürgen von Hagen.

in 1861 and Germany in 1871, where different cantons, regions or kingdoms finally accepted a single currency *after* they had become politically united. The inter-European unions, of which we shall examine the Latin Monetary Union (LMU), all failed for lack of political unity (Vanthoor, 1996: chs 3 and 4).

The Swiss monetary unification took a long time to come to fruition, and did so in the end by breaking the monetary links with France and centralising the note issue. Political unification in 1848 led to a single coin system for the whole of the confederation, but note issue was not included in the national pact. Despite the interference of the LMU, the single coinage worked acceptably well. But note issue was controlled by the cantons until the monopoly of paper money was vested in the Swiss National Bank in 1905. These notes were granted forced-currency status in 1914, but convertibility was restored in 1929. By now Swiss banknotes were well established and the country monetarily integrated.

Though the single currency in Italy included metal and paper, it took a long time for notes to be unified. Commercial banks competed in note issue, which at first had a ceiling imposed; then the ceiling could be exceeded as long as the extra issue was covered by metal. This of itself was a positive development for a country needing capital to grow. But what shook the system was the suspension of convertibility during the war with Austria and again after 1894, both measures induced by continued budget deficits. Vanthoor concludes that: 'the unification of paper money issuance failed in spite of political unity. ... The lack of monetary control was the result of the absence of effective mechanisms of cooperation rather than of there being more than one bank of issue' (ibid.: 20).

The LMU was created in 1865 and lasted in one form or another until 1927. Under the leadership of France, a common currency was established with Belgium, Switzerland, Italy and later Greece, whereby franc, lira and drachma coins were given equal weight and fineness. Spain took the step of issuing pesetas of the same definition but never joined.

Two difficulties troubled the LMU: the fact that it was in effect a bimetallist system, and the differing spending policies of its members. The exchange rate between silver and gold tacitly assumed in the treaty was the traditional one of 15.5:1. When silver started depreciating in the 1870s there was a rush to exchange fractional silver money for gold coins that were then melted down. Silver bullion was imported in large quantities to be minted, leading to an increase in inflation. The difficulty was corrected by stopping the minting of silver coins, especially of five-franc pieces, in 1878. This amounted to adopting the gold standard and reducing silver to the role of fractional money.

The second difficulty was less manageable. Italy resorted to printing inconvertible paper money to finance its war with Austria, its aim being to take over the Veneto, and Greece followed suit. This led to large exports of Italian and Greek silver coins to France and Switzerland, to be exchanged at par for paper money of better quality; then French and Swiss notes were brought back south to be exchanged at a premium for local paper. This kind of incident recurred during the history of the union and is in essence equivalent to a member of EMU taking advantage of the narrow spread under the single euro to issue excessive government debt.

EMU as an instrument to deepen European integration

Accepting that a currency readily usable in international

commercial transactions is very convenient, the question is whether one such money can be had without the political implications of the centralised, monopolistic kind. The answer is 'Yes' only if the value of the currency is established independently from the fiat of a government. This is the lesson of the Spanish monetary system in the seventeenth century, and of the gold standard of the nineteenth. But since today commodity money is unacceptable to sovereign issuers, which prefer fiat money, then the second-best solution is monetary competition. In the present day of fiat money and interfering governments, currencies will be national or, if issued by a number of like-minded states, will be organised along the lines of centralised national currencies. These monetary regimes, whatever the overt rules to which they are subject, will in the end malfunction. Until a new kind of commodity money can be organised, along the lines suggested by Kevin Dowd (1989: ch. 4), the only check to government abuse of money is competition among currencies that are not legal tender but are fully open to use by anyone. Even within the borders of a state or monetary union, the abolition of legal tender will make the centralisation of power and constitution of a centralised fiscal authority unnecessary for the acceptance of a currency. In Europe the aim ought to be, rather than monetary unification, monetary competition, helping keep a number of currencies sufficiently stable. International users will take account of its reliability and acceptability and of the existence of other candidate international currencies acting as a safety net. No legal tender or international agreements or political impositions of any kind are needed there. This is the lesson of Hayek's proposal to denationalise money (Hayek, 1976).

In contrast, it seems that a monetary union cannot last without the transfer of budgetary control to a central authority; that this central fiscal authority must allow for what has been called 'regional co-insurance';[4] and that regional co-insurance must not be stretched too far by great economic differences among the regions of the union.

For this last reason, the central authority must be able to stop members from applying imprudent expansionary policies. But such policies are not usually capricious. They answer the urgent needs of countries with sudden or chronic deficits due to a deficient tax system. Hence the union needs automatic transfer mechanisms from richer or booming regions to poorer or depressed ones. And these transfers must not be too large or the solidarity among members will be stretched too far.

From the experiences of currency unions related above, one may arrive at the following conclusions:

1   monetary integration has been successful in politically unified countries, but after long adaptation periods;
2   persistent budget deficits make an orthodox monetary policy difficult and lead to frictions in the financial markets;
3   inter-European monetary unions have all failed for lack of a central authority to coordinate money creation; to stop irresponsible public financing by constituent sovereign states; and to arrange a common fiscal system offering regions mutual co-insurance.

Vanthoor seems then to be justified in saying that 'the most important lesson was that monetary union is only sustainable and irreversible if it is embedded in a political union, in which

4   Eichengreen (1993), as cited in Vanthoor (1996: 125).

competences beyond the monetary sphere are also transferred to a supranational body'.

In view of this lesson from history, Vanthoor is led to question the solidity of EMU, seeing that European political unity is far from achieved. But he takes some comfort from the fact that 'EMU is underlain by political motives' and hopes that the logic of monetary unity will in this case foster political unification: 'EMU is the most suitable instrument to deepen European integration, as it may potentially develop its own dynamics from which the need for political union may arise … Unification will not proceed without some kind of incentive of a political nature' (Vanthoor, 1996: 133).

Indeed! But is there no other way to ease international transactions without increasing political control and centralisation?

The dangers of a single currency in the EU

When deciding whether sterling, the two kronas (and the Swiss franc) should be given up, we must try to imagine what the drawbacks could be of full EMU for the whole of Europe. A number of quasi-economic drawbacks have been indirectly mentioned, but the main dangers are of a constitutional kind.

Temptations in running the euro

If one takes the ECB and ECOFIN together as the monetary authority of EMU, a number of pitfalls appear whose existence makes one wary of the euro.

1 The political cycle: the traditional way of defining the political

cycle in a single state with one currency is to predict that there will be monetary expansion before, and contraction after, an election. Though the ECB is independent of the European Council and Commission and must not accommodate national governments, the pressures on the ECB to keep interest rates low will be continual: general elections in the different member states happen all the time, and there will always be complaints that monetary policy is too tight; and occasions for demanding contraction will be few and far between. Expansionary demands will be dressed up as efforts to counteract the cycle and foster growth.

2 The Growth and Stability Pact: there will have to be a redefinition of the pact to enforce fiscal discipline if the euro is to stand out against the dollar, a currency now buckling under the weight of public debt. The tendency seems to be going the other way, however, with talk of balancing the budget over the cycle and attempts by the drafters of the intended constitutional pact to have fiscal matters determined by majority voting only just thwarted. Indeed, the great temptation is to reinforce the legal-tender euro with a central European treasury. There is no talk of letting profligate member states go bankrupt.

3 Meddling with the exchange rate: the treaty establishing the ECB allows it to come to agreements with other monetary authorities to fix exchange rates, presumably with the dollar and the yen. Apart from the fact that domestic monetary policy will be made impossible for the ECB if exchanges do not float freely, international agreements to link the euro and other world currencies will hobble competition and give a free hand to governments wanting to tamper with the currency.

Constitutional aspects of the euro

Even more worrying are seven purely political aspects of the attempt to impose the euro on all member states.

1 Democratic deficit: in a democracy, changes in the economic constitution have to be understood, accepted and backed by the citizens. The euro was not chosen by the people of the various member states but imposed by governing elites. When the people have been directly consulted they have either approved the introduction of the new currency by a narrow majority or have rejected it outright. The British still have to give their assent.

2 Reform by sleight of hand: members states' politicians, instead of convincing their electorates that they should refrain from their populist habits, have a tendency to shift the blame for the pain that hard but necessary measures cause the general public on to the EU. The monetary orthodoxy and balanced budgets implicit in the euro project have not been fully explained to, and accepted by, the peoples of Europe. There is a danger that many ordinary European citizens will turn against the EU and the free economy as so many anti-globalisers are turning against the IMF and capitalism because of the unexpected sacrifices demanded by the market system.

3 Political integration by other means: the democratic deficit of the EU will be compounded by the undeclared political elements of the euro. The so-called Jean Monnet method is characterised by using economic reforms to further a political integration that dare not speak it name: the euro is another instance of this method, in that it is presented as a currency issued by a central bank that is

independent of all political pressures when in fact it is intended to cement European political unity.

4 Increased friction in the euro zone: the more divergent the economies in the non-optimal euro currency area the greater the occasions for disagreement on monetary policy among 25 or more member states. Trying to alleviate differences by transfer of structural and convergence funds has not worked in Germany, causing impatience in the West and disgruntlement in the East. With the occasion of the present expansion of the EU, aid from the richer member states to the poorer is being made more palatable by the erection of barriers to immigration and the imposition of the *acquis communautaire*. Under the guise of creating 'a level playing field', the capacity of the new members states to compete in the single market is thus reduced.

5 A smooth-functioning euro demands majority voting: I have argued above that modern economies riddled with sticky prices and uncompetitive wages need automatic fiscal stabilisers. These redistribution mechanisms can only appear in a federal fiscal system and resistance to a centralised treasury can only be broken by majority voting. The trend to restrict the use of the unanimity rule to make way for centralised regulation of other areas of economic activity is clearly noticeable in the proposed Constitutional Treaty: the charter of rights may lead to greater judicial intervention in labour markets; supervision may be moved from financial regulators to the ECB; the use of financial experts to develop flexible regulation for the financial industry included in the so-called 'Lamfalussy compromise' may be in danger (Hilton and Lascelles, 2003). Majority voting, by reducing the quorum

needed to create coalitions, will lead to the more highly regulated states agreeing among themselves to impose regulation on the less regulated (Vaubel, 2003).

6 Economics as a power game: politicians tend to think that the economy has to be governed if it is to function properly. They do not want to understand that the essence of a free economy is that it functions on its own within the framework of abstract laws. This attitude is understandable in the context of the EU, where political power can be useful to stop or to bring about intervention and regulation. The member states of the euro zone have created a 'Euro Group' in ECOFIN, to which Britain is not admitted. Maybe the best way for the UK, if it is to proceed along its own path towards prosperity, is precisely not to become a member of that pressure group.

7 A single European currency may reinforce the super-cartel character of the EU and become an obstacle to the progress of world free trade: if the euro contributes to the creation of a federal Europe, it may also consolidate the belief in the EU acting as a bloc in trade negotiations. Two of the fondest ideas of 'realistic' economists are that the paramount rule of commercial horse-trading is reciprocity, and that the best way to secure concessions from commercial partners is to act as a bloc. An economic and monetary union will tend to conceive of trade 'concessions' as defeats instead of as contributions to competitiveness. Professor Bhagwati (1999) was right in asking the question 'Building blocs or stumbling blocs?' when worrying about the effect of the proliferation of customs unions such as the EU, NAFTA, the Group of Rio and ASEAN on world free trade.

By keeping the pound sterling the UK will do the EU and the world a great deal of good, in helping avoid the consolidation of an economic and political cartel under the form of a federal Europe.

9 MONETARY COMPETITION AND FREE TRADE AS CONSTRAINTS ON POWER ABUSE

A stable currency should be a central part of the economic constitution of democratic countries. For the ordinary citizen, being as far as possible free from the inflation tax and the vagaries of the political cycle is a prerequisite of transparent democratic politics.

When the issue of money by merchants was taken over by princes, a private financial contract became a public constitutional compact: seignorage was granted in exchange for a stable currency. Sovereigns have been lax, however, in the performance of their part of this compact and have given in to the temptation of unduly profiting from a legal monopoly.

The economic ills flowing from variable inflation have pushed democratic opinion towards accepting some kind of institutional barrier to limit political pressure on central banks and to restrain the discretion of these banks in the issuing of money. Many countries have now made their central bank independent of government and the ECB has been made independent of the political structures of the EU. Independence is usually coupled with explicit rules governing the conduct of central bankers.

Two difficulties arise with this kind of arrangement, one internal to monetary policy and one external. As a part of their duties regarding the money they issue, central banks must not only maintain monetary stability but must also guarantee financial stability as lenders of last resort (Wood, 2002: 51–2): bailing out banks may imply bursts of liquidity and the creation of moral hazard. The external difficulty is how to make these independent central bankers accountable to some democratic authority. Methods include varying combinations of rules limiting money issue; transparency in the practice of monetary policy; and remote control by the finance minister or by parliament. Also, some powers affecting the value of money are being retained by governments, such as exchange rate policy or the issuing of public debt. But again, these residual powers may interfere with the proper conduct of central banks.

One of the well-tried weapons against monopoly and its possible abuses is free competition. It is all to the good that the ECB must work within a framework of rules with the end of making the euro more reliable. But something more is needed. In 1990, just before the Maastricht Treaty, James Buchanan proposed a policy of monetary competition with no legal tender which would have imposed the discipline of monetary competition on Europe's central bankers (Buchanan, 1990: 12–14). This policy was similar to that defended by John Major under the name of 'the common currency' for Europe – instead of the single currency. The citizens of Europe, proposed the British government of the time, would have a constitutional right to write contracts and pay taxes in the currency of their choice, including in ecus or euros if they so chose.

The chance of having the euro as a *common* currency and for people to choose between that and national money, rather than having a *single* European currency imposed by fiat, was missed. If the EU had accepted the British proposal of a 'parallel ecu', rules guaranteeing the stability of the common currency and its independence from European governments would have been a part of the offer to users of the money by the European bank. There would have been no need for constitutional rules to be made (and broken) by member states, and no need for a Growth and Stability Pact, since the euro would not have been seen as a possible instrument of state finance.

Competition among parallel currencies could have been an element of a fully open European Union, where tax and social services competition, commercial and cooperative rivalry, would have pointed the way towards a true single market with no outside barriers. Alas, dirigisme won the day.

There are two kinds of currency competition. One kind is that which existed in Scotland of the eighteenth and nineteenth centuries, when different private issuing banks competed with banknotes denominated in the same standard, the pound sterling. No local banker of last resort was needed, only spontaneous clearing arrangements and the publicity of exchange rates. The anchor of the system was demandable debt in the form of Bank of England banknotes convertible into gold on sight.[1] The other kind is the competition among issuers using different standards, a system which, with the low transactions costs brought about by financial globalisation, reduces the danger of systemic crises even more than the competition between different issues of money using the same standard. This latter is the system Buchanan proposed within Europe when the euro was on the drawing board. The condition was that 'citizens of Europe ... must be legally-constitutionally allowed to transact affairs, to make contracts enforceable

---

1   White (2000: 39). In the essay by Otmar Issing that White comments on, Dr Issing makes the far-fetched claim that the euro is a superior form of denationalised currency issued along the broad lines proposed by Hayek.

in their own courts, in monetary units issued by the central banks of *any* of the nation-states of the union, including the discharge of all monetary obligations, and specifically the payment of taxes to any and all political authorities' (ibid.: 13).

For Buchanan, this sort of arrangement would have closely resembled Hayek's competing-currencies scheme (Hayek, 1976). A system of open competing standards and currencies will find central bankers and the commercial banks of their club very sensitive to their clients starting to use another currency. True, the general public will react slowly to the debasement of the currency they are accustomed to using, since money is, as has often been remarked, a network good with a high cost for those who turn to another issuer. But currency competition need only tempt marginal financial transactors for 'alarm bells' to start ringing. In the course of time, the best-behaved money will prevail, following what is called the 'inverse Gresham's law'.

There is always the fear that competition will be a race to the bottom, a fear that experience has proved wrong time and again in different markets. For most goods and services, gainful competition is based on sustained quality, reputation and trust. Choice of jurisdiction will reveal preferences regarding public goods, since individuals will either 'vote with their feet' to move to preferred locations from the point of view of levels of taxation and social services, or trade and place their financial and real investments where they expect secure and gainful results (Tiebout, 1956). As regards foreign exchange markets, competitive devaluations, so prevalent in the 1930s with destructive results, are not sustainable without exchange controls.

In sum, my economic-constitutional argument is the following:

If the real economy is not fundamentally affected by which of many currencies transactors use, as long as those currencies are sound, the main argument for keeping the pound, the kronas and the Swiss franc in competition with the euro is that they impose a mutual discipline on their several central bankers and offer a variety of havens for ordinary people against unpredictable inflation.

But currency competition is not enough to create an open European economy of the sort that will guarantee individual economic rights. Buchanan argued for two constitutional rules, not one: a rule allowing Europeans to choose the currency they preferred for all their payments and contracts, and a rule allowing them to trade freely with all the world. 'The internal free trade area may be sufficiently large to capture most if not all of the scale advantages of an extended market. But freedom for external trade serves the equally important function of ensuring that internal political coalitions among majorities of the separate nation-states will not successfully exploit minorities, and especially as concentrated in particular member-units' (Buchanan, 1990: 16).

But this kind of Europe would have been precisely the sort that Patrick Minford said would make giving up sterling for the euro worthwhile: a euro embedded in a free-market Europe, playing a role similar to that of gold, with many convertible currencies around, in the golden era of globalisation from 1870 until World War I.

10 SUMMARY OF THE POLITICAL ARGUMENTS FOR AND AGAINST BRITAIN ADOPTING THE EURO

Now that the likely role of currency and institutional competition has been analysed, it is possible to compile a table with the main political points for and against keeping sterling: see Table 4.

1 and 2: The euro is primarily a political, not an economic, project. The creation of a European monetary union is an attempt to invert the historical order of things, whereby monetary unions did not succeed unless there was a single political authority to control free riders on the legal-tender imposition: the aim now is to use the need created by monetary union for political unity to create that political unity. Keeping the pound, the two kronas (and the Swiss franc) will slow down the drive towards federalism.

3 and 4: Peace in Europe has at least as much to do with US involvement in European affairs since 1943 as with France and Germany building the EU. The beneficent effects of American intervention are clearest in the fall of the Iron Curtain and the dissolution of the Soviet empire after the collapse of the Berlin Wall in 1989. The dangers for European unity do not come from a rekindling of the animosity between the French and the Germans, but from tensions caused by frictions over common policy, not least monetary policy.

Table 4 **Britain and the euro: political arguments for and against adoption**

Adopting the € throughout the EU to create a centralised currency union

1	The € a symbol for European unity
2	The logic of the € leads to majority voting and perhaps to a single federal authority
3	Renouncing national seignorage reduces the means to wage war, except by EU consent
4	A single currency avoids friction among member states caused by variable exchange rates
5	The € helps push unpopular reforms
6	Adopting the € would increase British influence in the EU and the 'Euro Group' where economic power is exercised
7	Protects the 'European' model of capitalism from short-term capital movements and currency speculation
8	Harmonisation and convergence make for a more united Europe
9	Helps the EU to speak with a single voice in WTO trade negotiations
10	By fostering economic centralisation, helps Europe become one of the world's main power blocs
11	Creates a counter-weight for the $ and for US power

5: Though convincing a reluctant electorate to accept reforms because they are demanded by the ECB and ECOFIN is a risky game, it may be working in some countries (not France and Germany): in these cases the euro should be kept and the rules obeyed. But the piecemeal method of mutual recognition of standards, also widely used to good effect in the EU, could be reinforced by a measure of monetary diversity.

Keeping the £, the kronas and the Swiss franc to maintain currency and institutional competition	*Balance*
The fight for the £ and other national currencies helps rally the critics of European federalism	£
The € is a means for political centralisation through the back door	£
Keeping sterling does not mean leaving the EU, where conflicts are resolved peacefully	=
Staying out helps avoid euro zone squabbles over the single monetary policy	£
Monetary variety works for mutual recognition of national standards	?
The £ fits in an economy based on competition within a framework of abstract rules, rather than on power games	£
Having a national currency fosters institutional competition and reinforces the discipline imposed by global capital movements	£
Leaves room for nations working for a leaner state and real economic freedom	£
May help create more variety, and perhaps reduce the weight of reciprocity, in trade negotiations	€
Maintaining the £ is conducive to preserving a strong Western Alliance	£
British autonomy based on the £ helps reduce the weight of Continental anti-Americanism	£

6 and 7: The forming of coalitions in the European Council might be curbed if some of the more important member states concentrated on creating conditions for keener competition: there is danger in hiding in a large currency area, where the consequences of financial misbehaviour are not immediately visited on the culprit.

8: Again, harmonisation and convergence can turn out to be a strategy of raising rivals' costs to the level of those of the more regulated.

9: Discussing the best way to accomplish world free trade would be the subject of another monograph, but it may be the case that Europe, by speaking with one voice at the Doha Round table, simplifies and speeds up negotiations.

10 and 11: Any reform endangering the Western Alliance should be counted as a step in the wrong direction.

It appears that keeping sterling wins on almost all counts politically. There are two types of monetary union. The first is based on a single money imposed by central authorities. Such a monetary union requires centralised political authority and, in the EU, that centralised political authority would not create the conditions necessary for a free European economy. The other form of 'monetary union' arises from the free choice of individuals predominantly using one out of a range of alternative currencies. The latter model does not require centralised political authority and is a better model for ensuring that monetary discipline is maintained.

11 CONCLUSION: IT'S ABOUT THE KIND OF EUROPE WE WANT

A treaty too far.

LADY THATCHER, ON MAASTRICHT

By keeping the pound while staying in the EU, by rejecting the euro and pushing Europe in a free-market direction, and by engaging the USA and committing everything to the next round of the WTO negotiations, Britain may be of more service to itself, Europe and humanity than by submitting to the Giscard d'Estaing programme of constitutional change.

Two views of the EU

The EU is a double-edged project. There is much good in it. It started as a project to make peace permanent in the heart of our continent, under the benevolent eye of our American allies. It has given a constitutional anchor to countries such as Spain, Portugal and Greece that have a past dominated by dictatorships and military coups (see Crespo MacLennan, 2000). It now provides a democratic haven for nations in central and eastern Europe that were subject to the rule of the Soviet empire. It may even help to bring Muslims in Turkey and around the Mediterranean nearer to Western liberalism. It has opened borders that separated people, brought down barriers that impeded the free flow of trade and finance, and has thus created new and welcome areas of competition.

There also are trends in the EU that are worrying for those of us who believe in individual liberty. Ordinary citizens have little say in the decisions taken by a remote elite of politicians and bureaucrats. The Commission is indeed a bureaucrat's paradise. The European Parliament has no real constituency as yet. The Court of Justice shows a clear federalist bias. The imposition of the Social Charter smacks of anti-competitive regulation hurting precisely those people it claims to protect. The Common Agricultural Policy harms the poor of the world and is only slowly being reformed. The commercial policies of the EU often lay barriers on the road to free trade. In sum, the EU suffers from an excess of collusion and collective action that increase the pay-off from lobbying and cartel activities, as compared with the pay-off from production (see Olson, 1982: ch. 3).

The Versailles constitutional project

The draft Constitutional Treaty prepared at the Versailles Convention has a worrying interventionist side to it. First, three-quarters of this text just subsumes existing rules and regulations accumulated over the years through treaty after treaty, with no reconsideration of their fitness in a globalised society: the opening of the EU to new members, which will let in some fresh air, is limited by the imposition on them to take on the whole of the *acquis communautaire*, which in fact limits their ability to compete with the overweight and over-regulated older members states.

This is not the place to examine this document in detail; suffice it to say that the text forgets the principal lesson of the US Constitution of 1787: the need to limit the present powers and future extension of government with checks and balances, not the least of which is the economic autonomy of private individuals.[1] Only four remarks need be made here about the character of this document.

Creating power versus limiting power

Traditionally, constitutions have been framed to limit power, not to concentrate it. A liberal constitution first establishes a sphere of freedom around each person, so that individuals, be they in authority or not, refrain from invading the rights of other individuals. That protected sphere includes the right to one's body, liberty and property, the freedom of contract, and the expectancy that promises will be fulfilled. This allows individuals room to plan and conduct their lives as they see fit under the protection of the law. Second, a constitution should define the participation of citizens in the governance of their country. Only then does a constitution address the organisation of collective action, by defining the machinery of justice, legislation and government and establishing a division of political power in society, so that a balance is struck between the need to take collective decisions and the avoidance of excessive concentration of authority.

The proposed treaty, however, does not adequately balance its centralising reforms with checks powerful enough to stop the drift towards an over-intrusiveness so characteristic of the modern state. There are new posts of president and foreign secretary of the European Union, the extension of majority voting, and a consid-

---

1   See all the main articles in *Economic Affairs*, 24(1), for an in-depth consideration of the new EU Constitution and a comparison with the US constitutional convention.

erable increase in the powers of the European Parliament. The object of all this is a better and more democratic governance of the 25-member Union. Mutual limitation and control among the different institutions will not disappear. But this smoother and more efficient governance could result in weaker barriers to officious executive action.

The draft Constitution does not take full advantage of the fact that the economic freedoms of the individual are a powerful barrier against undue political interference. It fails to mention private property, freedom of contract, free enterprise, workable competition and free trade in its opening and most solemn articles on the definition and object of the Union. Although these guarantees are variously mentioned in different parts of the Charter, they are not given their rightful place as essential elements of individual liberty.

Subsidiarity and proportionality versus individual autonomy

Freedom is not only preserved by the horizontal division of power, however, but by vertical devolution to lower layers of authority, to the organisations of civil society, and especially to the individual. The proposed Charter is not unaware of the need to set up firewalls to limit excessive intervention from on high. It expands on the traditional concept of 'subsidiarity' by adding to it a demand for 'proportionality' in the measures taken by EU institutions. Also, national parliaments would be empowered to take EU institutions to court if subsidiarity and proportionality were infringed. But all these precautions appear nugatory when the list of areas designated for EU action is examined. The EU is granted control not only over the establishment of the internal market, but also over economic, monetary and competition policy; employment and social policy; economic, social and territorial cohesion; agriculture and fisheries; the environment; consumer protection; transport; trans-European networks; and research and technological development (not forgetting Giscard d'Estaing's space exploration project). The EU may also take coordinating, complementary or supporting action in public health, industry, culture, education, vocational training, youth and sport, civil protection and administrative cooperation.

This draft Treaty, by giving the institutions of the EU such a wide remit for action and intervention, fails to use the principal form of devolution in a free society: devolution to the individual rather than to layers of public organisations. The reliance on subsidiarity instead of individual autonomy as the barrier against power abuse shows a deep misunderstanding of the causes of the expansion of the state in modern society.

Harmonisation versus competition

It has been the practice of the EU to try to tackle the perceived problems caused by varying degrees of development, dissimilar national legislation and regulation, and different levels of taxation, through harmonisation. Only in despair of making headway on the harmonisation agenda has mutual recognition of national standards been applied, and this mostly in the fields of company law and financial regulation.

The choice of harmonisation rather than competition as the path towards the single market shows a lack of confidence in allowing individuals to exercise their economic freedoms under the legal regime of their choosing among those of Europe's member states. Mutual recognition of member states' legal arrangements would lead to spontaneous convergence through jurisdictional competition.

The Convention on the whole showed a diffident attitude towards personal and jurisdictional competition. The proposed text sets out the central objectives of the Union as being, among other things, 'a Europe of sustainable development based on balanced economic growth; a social market economy, highly competitive and aiming at full employment and social progress; and with a high level of protection and improvement of the quality of the environment'.

First, 'a highly competitive economy' is not the same as 'an economy with a high degree of competition'. The text seems to conceive of the EU as a business corporation that must sell its products and services aggressively to the rest of the world. This is traditional mercantilism. An economy is not a limited company: it is made up of people and businesses buying and selling in pursuit of their interests, in a context of free competition and cooperation. In fact, 'an economy' does not exist, except in the sense of being a legal and institutional framework for the activity of individuals and businesses.

Second, the text is politically correct to a fault. Fashionable concepts, such as 'sustainable development' and 'environmental protection', the contradictory aims of 'balanced economic growth' and a 'highly competitive economy', and pious hopes for 'full employment' and 'social progress' cannot hide a misunderstanding of what competition can do for society.

The EU and free trade: building blocks or stumbling blocks?

In spite of the forces shaping globalisation, in the fields of transport, communications, finance and culture, the nation-states, special interest groups, trade unions and industrial lobbies are putting up a rearguard fight to stop the increase in free trade. The position of the EU in matters of trade is ambiguous as set out in the proposed Charter.

On the one hand, the Common Market has been a force for lifting protectionist barriers among member states. The single market in such a large trading area as the EU has undoubtedly contributed to the extraordinary economic growth enjoyed by Europeans since the signing of the Treaty of Rome.

On the other hand, the strengthening and widening of the European club reinforce the trend towards a world divided into trade blocs. As a recent World Bank report points out (2001: 1), 'more than one third of world trade takes place within regional integration agreements'. In a world where trade blocs are on the increase, many Europeans think it would be artless to give up the monetary, economic, political and commercial means to keeping one's fate in one's own hands. In such a world, speaking with one voice may get one better deals in negotiations.

Behind this attitude lies the idea that any opening of one's markets must be reciprocated by an opening up of the market of one's trading partner. This is a mistaken but common view. Pandering to it plays into the hands of protectionists the world over, with especially harmful effects on the poorer countries, where taking trade out of the hands of governments would foster competition, help attract foreign investment and strengthen market institutions.

Sterling as a lever for competition and personal freedom

Many critics of the British government's plan to give up sterling for the euro do not deal with the essence of the question. The purpose of keeping sterling is not to defend monetary or political sovereignty but to contribute to personal freedom through economic and jurisdictional competition.

Those who argue in terms of sovereignty, wishing either to keep sovereignty within the nation-state or to transfer it to the EU, would think that at the heart of the case defended in this paper there are two inconsistencies:

- if, as long as it is stable, the currency is not a life-and-death question for the real economy, as is argued in this essay, then why is the euro such a big issue?
- if classical liberals incline towards internationalism, then how could we prefer a national currency rather than the euro, and prefer national states to a European federation?

It must be clear now that the first inconsistency is merely apparent. Keeping sterling and other national currencies alongside the euro will foster monetary competition as a check on central bankers' misbehaviour, so often seen in history. The very forces of competition will weed out those currencies that do not fulfil the needs of transactors. And monetary competition will become a beachhead for the sort of jurisdictional competition that allows individuals to choose the most propitious environment for their personal life plan and their communal endeavours. As such monetary competition will benefit both the UK and the euro zone.

The second apparent inconsistency can also be explained.

European liberals are internationalists, despite their resistance to much of what is being done in Europe in the name of creating a supra-national power lording over Europe. Many good Europeans are unhappy about the kind of Union being built in Europe and imposed on the nations now entering. They fear that a large coalition of centralisers is intending to vest sovereignty in European institutions, rather than devise checks and balances to limit their powers. They are concerned by the insistence of the defenders of the euro on harmonising rules, regulations and taxes, rather than having the different member states compete and be allowed to better discover forms of governance for themselves. They think that subsidiarity and proportionality are a weak remedy for the kind of bureaucratic control and high-handed interference for which Brussels is renowned. They fear that many Euro-enthusiasts do not see the free market as a privileged sphere of individual autonomy. They grow impatient with the commercial policy of the EU bloc that insists on reciprocity before opening up markets to alien trade and investment. In sum, they reject the mode of governance touted by the conventions of Versailles, more in the spirit of Robespierre than that of Madison.

From our discussion, we can see that a genuine free-market economic position on the euro leads to an ambiguous decision. Certainly, the UK government tests are not the relevant ones. Politics is key to the decision on whether to adopt the euro. It is not the politics of 'influence', of 'sovereignty' or of 'solidarity', however, but the politics of ensuring competition between institutions so that they serve the people they are intended to serve. By keeping sterling the UK imposes a competitive discipline on the ECB. This approach can be expanded to other areas of lawmaking, regulation and jurisdictional competition.

Now that both the euro and the Constitution are to be put to a popular vote, the British people have a chance to stop the drift towards centralisation in the EU. By refusing to give up sterling and rejecting the new Constitution, Britain will once again be battling for the freedom of Europe.

REFERENCES

Balassa, B. (1964), 'The Purchasing Power Parity Doctrine: a reappraisal', *Journal of Political Economy*, 72: 584–96.

Barrios, S. and Lucio, J. J. (2001), *Economic Integration and Regional Business Cycles: evidence from the Iberian Region*, FEDEA Working Paper no. 2001-17.

Bernal, A-M. (ed.) (2000), *Dinero, moneda y crédito en la monarquía hispánica*, Madrid: Marcial Pons – ICO.

Bhagwati, J. (1999), 'Introduction', in J. Bhagwati, P. Krisna and A. Panagariya, *Trading Blocs. An Alternative Approach to Analyzing Preferential Trade Agreements*, Cambridge, MA: MIT Press.

Bordo, M. and Jonung, L. (2000), *Lessons for EMU from the History of Monetary Unions*, London: IEA.

Buchanan, J. M. (1990), 'Europe's Constitutional Opportunity', in Buchanan et al., *Europe's Constitutional Future*, London: IEA.

Buchanan, J. M. and Wagner, R. E. (1977), *Democracy in Deficit: the political legacy of Lord Keynes*, vol. 8 of *The Collected Works of James M. Buchanan*, Indianapolis, IN: Liberty Fund.

Buiter, W. H. and Grafe, C. (2003), 'EMU or Ostrich', contribution to *Submissions on EMU from Leading Academics*, in HM Treasury (2003).

Castañeda, J. (2003), 'Propuesta de una regla de emisión para el Banco Central Europeo: de la estabilidad de precios a la estabilidad monetaria', doctoral thesis, Madrid: Universidad Autónoma.

Crespo MacLennan, J. (2000), *Spain and the Process of European Integration*, London: Palgrave.

Dowd, K. (1989), *The State and the Monetary System*, New York: Philip Allan.

Economist (2002), 'Euro Referendum: Rushing towards Europe', 18 May, p. 39.

Eichengreen, B. (1993), 'European Monetary Unification', in *Journal of Economic Literature*, 31(3): 1,321–57.

Eltis, W. (2000), 'Is EMU Sustainable without Political Union?', in Bordo and Jonung (2000), pp. 53–58.

European Community Commission (1990), 'One Market, One Money', in *European Economy*, 44.

Febrero, R. (1998), 'La nueva macroeconomía clásica y sus consecuencias para la formulación de la política económica', Working Paper no. 9811, Madrid: Facultad de Ciencias Económicas y Empresariales, Universidad Complutense.

Ferguson, N. (2001), *The Cash Nexus. Money and power in the modern world, 1700–2000*, London: Penguin Books.

Financial Times (2001), 'Swedish currency falls out of favour', 22 August.

Foreign Trade, published by the UK Trade Department.

Friedman, M. (1959), *A Program for Monetary Stability*, New York: Fordham University Press.

Friedman, M. (1976), 'Nobel Lecture: Inflation and Unemployment', *Journal of Political Economy*, 85: 451–72.

Friedman, M. and Schwartz, A. J. (1963), *A Monetary History of the United States, 1867–1960*, Princeton University Press.

García Guerra, E. (2000), 'Las decisiones monetarias de la monarquía castellana del siglo XVII y su incidencia en el funcionamiento del crédito privado', in Bernal (2000), pp. 575–92.

Goodhart, C. A. E. (1995), 'The Political Economy of Monetary Union', in Kennen, P. B. (ed.), *The Macroeconomics of the Open Economy*, Princeton University Press.

De Grauwe, P. (2000), *Economics of Monetary Union*, 4th edn, Oxford University Press.

De Grauwe, P. (2004), 'America's Strength Is the Eurozone's Problem', *Financial Times*, 8 January.

Hayek, F. A. (1976 [1978]), *Denationalisation of Money*, Hobart Paper no. 10, London: IEA.

Heller, P. (2003), *Who Will Pay: coping with ageing societies, climate change, and other long-term fiscal challenges*, Washington, DC: IMF.

Hess, G. D. and Shin, K. (1997), 'International and Intranational Business Cycles', *Oxford Review of Economic Policy*, XIII(3): 93–109.

Hilton, A. and Lascelles, D. (2003), 'The New Treaty's Threat to European Finance', *Financial Times*, 12 December.

Hirshman, A. O. (1970), *Exit, Voice and Loyalty: responses to decline in firms, organizations and states*, Harvard University Press.

HM Treasury (2003), *UK membership of the single currency. An assessment of the five economic tests*, Cm. 5776.

Jasay, A. de (1985), *The State*, Oxford: Blackwell.

Kennen, P. B. (1969), 'The Theory of Optimum Currency Areas: an Eclectic View', in Mundell, R. A. and Swoboda, A. K. (eds),

Monetary Problems of the International Economy, University of Chicago Press, pp. 41–60.

Krugman, P. (1991), 'Policy Problems of a Monetary Union', in de Grauwe, P. and Papademos, L. (eds), *The European Monetary System in the 1990s*, London: Longman.

Lamfalussy et al. (2001), *Final Report of the Committee of Wise Men*, http://europe.eu.int/comm/internal_market/en/finances/general/lamfalussyen.pdf.

Legrain, P. (2002), 'The Trouble with Sterling', *Financial Times*, 19 August.

Lindsey, B. (2002), *Against the Dead Hand. The Uncertain Struggle for Global Capitalism*, New York: John Wiley.

Lucas, R. E., Jr (1972), 'Expectations and the Neutrality of Money', *Journal of Economic Theory*, IV: 103–24.

Lucas, R. E., Jr (1976), 'Economic Policy Evaluation: a critique', *Carnegie-Rochester Conference Series on Public Policy*, 1: 19–46.

Lucas, R. E., Jr (1980), 'Rules, Discretion, and the Role of the Economic Advisor', in Fisher, S. (ed.), *Rational Expectations and Economic Policy*, University of Chicago Press, pp. 199–200.

McKinnon, R. I. (1963), 'Optimum Currency Areas', *American Economic Review*, 53: 717–24.

Minford, P. (2002a), *Should Britain Join the Euro. The Chancellor's Five Tests Examined*, London: IEA.

Minford, P. (2002b), 'The Euro and the Five Tests: some brief notes on the costs and benefits of EMU to the UK economy', contribution to *Submissions on EMU from Leading Academics*, in HM Treasury (2003).

Mundell, R. (1960), 'The Monetary Dynamics of International Adjustments under Fixed and Flexible Exchange Rates', *Quarterly Journal of Economics*.

Mundell, R. A. (1961), 'A Theory of Optimum Currency Areas', *American Economic Review*, 51: 657–65.

Mundell, R. A. (2000), Introduction to Bordo and Jonung (2000).

Mundell, R. A. (2002), contribution to *Submissions on EMU from Leading Academics*, in HM Treasury (2003).

Muth, J. F. (1961), 'Rational Expectations and the Theory of Price Movements', *Econometrica*, 29(3): 315–35.

Olson, M. (1982), *The Rise and Decline of Nations: economic growth, stagflation and social rigidities*, New Haven, CT: Yale University Press.

ONS (Office for National Statistics) (2002), *United Kingdom Balance of Payments* (The Pink Book).

Ricardo, D. (1817), *Principles of Political Economy and Taxation*, vol. I of *The Works and Correspondence of ...*, Cambridge University Press, 1962.

Rose, A. K. (2000), 'EMU's Potential Effect on British Trade: a Quantitative Assessment', a report for Britain in Europe.

Samuelson, P. (1964), 'Theoretical Notes on Trade Problems', *Review of Economics and Statistics*, 46: 145–64.

de Santiago Fernández, J. (2000), *Política monetaria en Castilla durante el siglo XVII*, Valladolid: Junta de Castilla y León.

Sanz Ayán, C. (2000), 'Hombres de negocios y suspensiones de pagos en el siglo XVII', in Bernal (2000), pp. 727–50.

Sargent, T. J. (1987), 'Rational Expectations', in Eatwell et al. (eds), *The New Palgrave Dictionary of Economics*, London: Macmillan.

Savin, N. E. (1987), 'Rational Expectations: econometric implications', in Eatwell et al. (eds), *The New Palgrave Dictionary of Economics*, London: Macmillan.

Schwartz, P. (1997), *Back from the Brink*, London: IEA.

Skidelsky, R. (2001), 'The Politics of Euro Economics', *Financial Times*, 23 January.

Smith, A. (1776), *An Inquiry into the Nature and Causes of the Wealth of Nations*, republished 1976 in the Glasgow Edition of *The Works and Correspondence of Adam Smith*, Oxford: Clarendon Press.

Tiebout, C. M. (1956), 'A Pure Theory of Local Expenditures', *Journal of Political Economy*, 50: 416–24.

Vanthoor, W. F. V. (1996), *European Monetary Union since 1848. A Political and Historical Analysis*, Cheltenham: Edward Elgar.

Vaubel, R. (2003), 'Europe's Faster Route to Too Much Regulation', *Financial Times*, 14 November.

White, L. H. (1999), *The Theory of Monetary Institutions*, Oxford: Blackwell.

White, L. H. (2000), 'Commentary', in Issing et al., *Hayek, Currency Competition and European Monetary Union*, London: IEA.

Wood, G. E. (2002), 'Commentary', in Otmar Issing, *Should We Have Faith in Central Banks?*, London: IEA.

World Bank (2000), *Trade Blocs*, Policy Research Report published for the World Bank by Oxford University Press.

Wynne, M. and Koo, J. (1997), *Business Cycles under Monetary Union*, Federal Reserve Bank of Dallas Working Paper no. 97-07.

Yeager, L. B. (ed.) (1997), *The Fluttering Veil. Essays on Monetary Disequilibrium*, Indianapolis, IN: Liberty Fund.

INDEX

Page numbers in *italic* refer to Tables, Figures, Boxes and their captions. Page numbers followed by (n) refer to footnotes.

ABOUT THE IEA

The Institute is a research and educational charity (No. CC 235 351), limited by guarantee. Its mission is to improve understanding of the fundamental institutions of a free society with particular reference to the role of markets in solving economic and social problems.

The IEA achieves its mission by:

- a high-quality publishing programme
- conferences, seminars, lectures and other events
- outreach to school and college students
- brokering media introductions and appearances

The IEA, which was established in 1955 by the late Sir Antony Fisher, is an educational charity, not a political organisation. It is independent of any political party or group and does not carry on activities intended to affect support for any political party or candidate in any election or referendum, or at any other time. It is financed by sales of publications, conference fees and voluntary donations.

In addition to its main series of publications the IEA also publishes a quarterly journal, *Economic Affairs*, and has two specialist programmes – Environment and Technology, and Education.

The IEA is aided in its work by a distinguished international Academic Advisory Council and an eminent panel of Honorary Fellows. Together with other academics, they review prospective IEA publications, their comments being passed on anonymously to authors. All IEA papers are therefore subject to the same rigorous independent refereeing process as used by leading academic journals.

IEA publications enjoy widespread classroom use and course adoptions in schools and universities. They are also sold throughout the world and often translated/reprinted.

Since 1974 the IEA has helped to create a world-wide network of 100 similar institutions in over 70 countries. They are all independent but share the IEA's mission.

Views expressed in the IEA's publications are those of the authors, not those of the Institute (which has no corporate view), its Managing Trustees, Academic Advisory Council members or senior staff.

Members of the Institute's Academic Advisory Council, Honorary Fellows, Trustees and Staff are listed on the following page.

The Institute gratefully acknowledges financial support for its publications programme and other work from a generous benefaction by the late Alec and Beryl Warren.

The Institute of Economic Affairs
2 Lord North Street, Westminster, London SW1P 3LB
Tel: 020 7799 8900
Fax: 020 7799 2137
Email: iea@iea.org.uk
Internet: iea.org.uk

Other papers recently published by the IEA include:

WHO, What and Why?

Transnational Government, Legitimacy and the World Health Organization
Roger Scruton
Occasional Paper 113; ISBN 0 255 36487 3
£8.00

The World Turned Rightside Up

A New Trading Agenda for the Age of Globalisation
John C. Hulsman
Occasional Paper 114; ISBN 0 255 36495 4
£8.00

The Representation of Business in English Literature

Introduced and edited by Arthur Pollard
Readings 53; ISBN 0 255 36491 1
£12.00

Anti-Liberalism 2000

The Rise of New Millennium Collectivism
David Henderson
Occasional Paper 115; ISBN 0 255 36497 0
£7.50

Capitalism, Morality and Markets

Brian Griffiths, Robert A. Sirico, Norman Barry & Frank Field

Readings 54; ISBN 0 255 36496 2

£7.50

A Conversation with Harris and Seldon

Ralph Harris & Arthur Seldon

Occasional Paper 116; ISBN 0 255 36498 9

£7.50

Malaria and the DDT Story

Richard Tren & Roger Bate

Occasional Paper 117; ISBN 0 255 36499 7

£10.00

A Plea to Economists Who Favour Liberty: Assist the Everyman

Daniel B. Klein

Occasional Paper 118; ISBN 0 255 36501 2

£10.00

The Changing Fortunes of Economic Liberalism

Yesterday, Today and Tomorrow

David Henderson

Occasional Paper 105 (new edition); ISBN 0 255 36520 9

£12.50

The Global Education Industry

Lessons from Private Education in Developing Countries
James Tooley
Hobart Paper 141 (new edition); ISBN 0 255 36503 9
£12.50

Saving Our Streams

The Role of the Anglers' Conservation Association in Protecting English and Welsh Rivers
Roger Bate
Research Monograph 53; ISBN 0 255 36494 6
£10.00

Better Off Out?

The Benefits or Costs of EU Membership
Brian Hindley & Martin Howe
Occasional Paper 99 (new edition); ISBN 0 255 36502 0
£10.00

Buckingham at 25

Freeing the Universities from State Control
Edited by James Tooley
Readings 55; ISBN 0 255 36512 8
£15.00

Lectures on Regulatory and Competition Policy
Irwin M. Stelzer
Occasional Paper 120; ISBN 0 255 36511 X
£12.50

Misguided Virtue
False Notions of Corporate Social Responsibility
David Henderson
Hobart Paper 142; ISBN 0 255 36510 1
£12.50

HIV and Aids in Schools
The Political Economy of Pressure Groups and Miseducation
Barrie Craven, Pauline Dixon, Gordon Stewart & James Tooley
Occasional Paper 121; ISBN 0 255 36522 5
£10.00

The Road to Serfdom
The Reader's Digest *condensed version*
Friedrich A. Hayek
Occasional Paper 122; ISBN 0 255 36530 6
£7.50

Bastiat's *The Law*

Introduction by Norman Barry

Occasional Paper 123; ISBN 0 255 36509 8

£7.50

A Globalist Manifesto for Public Policy

Charles Calomiris

Occasional Paper 124; ISBN 0 255 36525 X

£7.50

Euthanasia for Death Duties

Putting Inheritance Tax Out of Its Misery

Barry Bracewell-Milnes

Research Monograph 54; ISBN 0 255 36513 6

£10.00

Liberating the Land

The Case for Private Land-use Planning

Mark Pennington

Hobart Paper 143; ISBN 0 255 36508 X

£10.00

IEA Yearbook of Government Performance 2002/2003

Edited by Peter Warburton
Yearbook 1; ISBN 0 255 36532 2
£15.00

Britain's Relative Economic Performance, 1870–1999

Nicholas Crafts
Research Monograph 55; ISBN 0 255 36524 1
£10.00

Should We Have Faith in Central Banks?

Otmar Issing
Occasional Paper 125; ISBN 0 255 36528 4
£7.50

The Dilemma of Democracy

Arthur Seldon
Hobart Paper 136 (reissue); ISBN 0 255 36536 5
£10.00

Capital Controls: a 'Cure' Worse Than the Problem?

Forrest Capie

Research Monograph 56; ISBN 0 255 36506 3

£10.00

The Poverty of 'Development Economics'

Deepak Lal

Hobart Paper 144 (reissue); ISBN 0 255 36519 5

£15.00

Should Britain Join the Euro?

The Chancellor's Five Tests Examined

Patrick Minford

Occasional Paper 126; ISBN 0 255 36527 6

£7.50

Post-Communist Transition: Some Lessons

Leszek Balcerowicz

Occasional Paper 127; ISBN 0 255 36533 0

£7.50

A Tribute to Peter Bauer

John Blundell et al.

Occasional Paper 128; ISBN 0 255 36531 4

£10.00

Employment Tribunals

Their Growth and the Case for Radical Reform

J. R. Shackleton

Hobart Paper 145; ISBN 0 255 36515 2

£10.00

Fifty Economic Fallacies Exposed

Geoffrey E. Wood

Occasional Paper 129; ISBN 0 255 36518 7

£12.50

A Market in Airport Slots

Keith Boyfield (editor), David Starkie, Tom Bass & Barry Humphreys

Readings 56; ISBN 0 255 36505 5

£10.00

Money, Inflation and the Constitutional Position of the Central Bank

Milton Friedman & Charles A. E. Goodhart

Readings 57; ISBN 0 255 36538 1

£10.00

railway.com

Parallels between the early British railways and the ICT revolution
Robert C. B. Miller
Research Monograph 57; ISBN 0 255 36534 9
£12.50

The Regulation of Financial Markets

Edited by Philip Booth & David Currie
Readings 58; ISBN 0 255 36551 9
£12.50

Climate Alarmism Reconsidered

Robert L. Bradley Jr
Hobart Paper 146; ISBN 0 255 36541 1
£12.50

Government Failure: E. G. West on Education

Edited by James Tooley & James Stanfield
Occasional Paper 130; ISBN 0 255 36552 7
£12.50

Waging the War of Ideas

John Blundell
Second edition
Occasional Paper 131; ISBN 0 255 36547 0
£12.50

Corporate Governance: Accountability in the Marketplace
Elaine Sternberg
Second edition
Hobart Paper 147; ISBN 0 255 36542 X
£12.50

The Land Use Planning System
Evaluating Options for Reform
John Corkindale
Hobart Paper 148; ISBN 0 255 36550 0
£10.00

Economy and Virtue
Essays on the Theme of Markets and Morality
Edited by Dennis O'Keeffe
Readings 59; ISBN 0 255 36504 7
£12.50

Free Markets Under Siege
Cartels, Politics and Social Welfare
Richard A. Epstein
Occasional Paper 132; ISBN 0 255 36553 5
£10.00

Unshackling Accountants

D. R. Myddelton

Hobart Paper 149; ISBN 0 255 36559 4

£12.50

To order copies of currently available IEA papers, or to enquire about availability, please contact:

Lavis Marketing
IEA orders
FREEPOST LON21280
Oxford OX3 7BR

Tel: 01865 767575
Fax: 01865 750079
Email: orders@lavismarketing.co.uk

The IEA also offers a subscription service to its publications. For a single annual payment, currently £40.00 in the UK, you will receive every title the IEA publishes across the course of a year, invitations to events, and discounts on our extensive back catalogue. For more information, please contact:

Subscriptions
The Institute of Economic Affairs
2 Lord North Street
London SW1P 3LB

Tel: 020 7799 8900
Fax: 020 7799 2137
Website: www.iea.org.uk